Endorsements page

HEART
CENTERED
BUSINESS

Heart
Centered

Business

MARK SILVER

Wildhouse
Publications

Design by Cambridge Creative Group

Published by Wildhouse Publications, an imprint of Wildhouse Publishing
(www.WildhousePublishing.com). No part of this book may be repro-
duced in any manner without the written permission from the publisher,
except in brief quotations embodied in critical articles or reviews. Contact
info@wildhousepublishing.com.

Printed in the USA

ISBN: 978-1-961741-02-7

Dedication

Contents

Acknowledgements

Bismillah ir-rahman ir-rahim.

According to the Sufis, appreciation is a Divine quality, one that we can fill with and express, but can't create. I feel humbled in that way by all the generosity, good will, and support showered upon me by so many.

First, I give thanks to the One. All that is written here that carries truth is from the Oneness, and any mistakes or omissions are my own. I ask Allah to shower all the prophets with blessings, love, and greetings of peace: peace be upon them all.

To Holly Glaser, my wife and companion and friend, who has been with me since 1994, I have such a deep and abiding love and gratitude for you. You have been my companion of truth and sincerity. You have mentored and taught me in many ways, and I'm grateful you're a full partner in Heart of Business. Your editing and feedback is a tremendously huge part of this book, and it cannot be overstated how much your thoughts and wisdom and heart have contributed to the work in general and this book in particular.

To my boys, Sam and David, who have shown patience and maturity while I've worked on this book, and also brought joy and silliness and games and love and care in uncounted ways. And also impatience with me, which has helped me stay balanced and not too deeply disappeared into work. Bless you and thank you.

To my parents Rae and Steve Silver, who taught me so much about life and love, family, and commitment. About entrepreneurship and business and how to care for customers long-term. And how to care long-term for a loving relationship.

I have deep gratitude for the blessings of the Shaddhiliyya Sufi lineage as transmitted to me by my sheikh, Muhammad Sa'id al-Jamal ar-Rifa'i ash-Shadhuli, who has returned to Allah, and may Allah be pleased with him. Sidi, as his students referred to him, was and is a deep blessing to my heart and life.

To the team at Wildhouse Press, especially Andrea Hollingsworth, who first invited me to submit a proposal for this book, then was such a caring and exacting editor to help bring it to life. For a first experience working with a publisher, you've made it a joy.

To the Heart of Business team, including Teresa who left the team to further pursue her own business partway through the writing of this book, and Criselda, our newest addition. Cathy, Tanya, Anni, Amy and Shelly, as well as Greg and Casper and Jessica. You all have been a rock of support in making Heart of Business run with such care and love.

To the members of the Heart of Business Learning Community, and so many of my own private clients, whose stories, in pieces and made anonymous, lie within these pages. Thank you for your vulnerability and willingness to bring your precious dream of a business to us and this work.

To Sufis who have been the earth for me, teachers to me, and friends and beloveds on the path with me, I'm so grateful for your hearts and presence in this dunya. Sarah Sabrina N'Diaye, Jamil and Na'ima Bastress, Latifa Shay, Ibrahim Jaffe, Wadude and Nura Laird, Salima Adelstein, Camila Widad Kraemer, Fawzia al-Rawi.

To my colleagues and friends Molly Gordon, Eric Klein, Michael Bungay-Stanier, and Jennifer Louden. We were in a brain trust together for fifteen years, and although that has come to an end, I cherish what you all gave me, how we contributed to each other's lives and businesses over that time. Love and friendship and care in the world of business.

To friends and teachers, some of whom I've never met in person, nevertheless whose presence and love and care has impacted me more than perhaps you might realize. I've learned deeply about social justice, about business in these strange times, about collective care, and so much more from you all. Nicole Lee, Ericka Hines, Tad Hargrave (my brother of the heart), Andrea J. Lee, Desiree Adaway, Chris Zydel, Leela Sinha, Dusti Arab, Yollana Shore, Crys Wood, Barrington Salmon, Paul Zelizer, Kerra Bolton, Rachel Alexandria, Pam Slim, Robert Middleton, Staci Jordan Shelton, Michele Green, and Gareth Higgins.

To our friends of the heart here in central Pennsylvania, Somers, Jake, Lily, Morgan, Quinn, Sonders, Evan, Kendra, Tyler, Emily, and the larger Compton clan who held our family so well through the difficult years of being new in a place during a pandemic. You have woven us into a larger community of family, community, regenerative agriculture, farming, and earth care that is at the heart of what we so deeply care about.

To all on the path of the Love, whatever form it takes. We all need each other so desperately; if any are missing, we are not complete.

Why This Book Exists

In the more than twenty years I've worked with clients on their businesses, the most common reason I've seen people stop is to avoid something that feels out of integrity. If it compromises their sense of truth, goodness, and wholeness, they just won't do it.

Business culture is so toxic, and affects us so profoundly, that many people struggle to create an ethical business that feels great to their heart and also thrives.

I see the disconnect all the time, when people with incredible skills and huge hearts nevertheless get caught up unconsciously in recreating terrible scorched-earth business and marketing strategies. Or, more commonly, they avoid marketing at all, and their business stagnates.

This book exists—my work exists—because healing is necessary in the world of business and in individuals who wish to be in business.

I say *healing* quite deliberately because strategies, tactics, even working on changing mindsets and beliefs, don't quite get at what I think many of us intuitively know is really needed.

What Is Healing?

Again, because of a dysfunctional culture, many are reluctant to use the word *healing*. Or, when they do, they often think of it as an individual process. In a sense, this is correct: there are individual aspects to the journey.

But healing, as my teachers taught me, is about melting the illusion of separation. It's about coming into wholeness. Yes, that includes individual wholeness. But it also means a collective wholeness.

This wholeness in ourselves and between each other means we do things that support thriving. And we do this without harming others—including people, animals, and the world around us, from which we aren't separate.

That wholeness arises out of love. In this culture, love is often talked about as soft, nice, comforting. But the Sufis, those mystical servants of the heart, talk about the annihilating power of love.

Love, if it were unleashed with strength, wisdom, and compassion, would annihilate the world of business as it is, turning it into something entirely different. If Love had its way, business could be part of a culture and society that lifts us up and serves us all.

That's what I believe is needed. An annihilation that heals our hearts, heals the world of business, heals us in our relationships around how we make our livelihood and share our gifts in the world.

As much as we need collective healing, we also, at the same time, need personal healing. This book will help you walk into personal healing around business in a way that supports collective healing.

We do this healing by discerning between what is truly harmful, which we avoid, and what is uncomfortable, where we can lean in and find the love that has been hidden or distorted. This is how we learn and implement the details of developing a business that is an expression of that love.

How to Use This Book

Before it was a book, the content on these pages was a course that thousands of participants have moved through. Before it was a course, most of the individual pieces had been worked with many times in other programs and individually with clients.

I have found that, in general, the topics in this book build on each other. So for most people, reading it through in order is a powerful way to do it. But you don't have to. Engaging the material in an "a la carte" way is just fine too.

The chapters include practical exercises to help deepen your understanding and end-of-chapter summaries to help solidify the concepts.

Chapters 1, 2, and 3 are explicitly about healing. We begin by focusing on healing your relationship with business and money, and with learning to trust yourself. It will be tempting to jump ahead into the more "practical" chapters on marketing and the elements of business. And that's fine—you can jump ahead.

However, what I've observed is that the toxicity we've all soaked up from the culture makes it hard to take on the more practical pieces without hurting yourself or hurting others. It makes the work much harder, less fun, and less nourishing.

Go through the first three chapters and you'll have a foundation of love, connection, and, hopefully, a transformed understanding of business and money that will make the following chapters much easier and more joyful.

Chapters 4 and 5 present a developmental model for growing microbusinesses. Most of our clients think their businesses are broken or not working in some way. When they get that their businesses are just developing, it brings profound relief.

There are so many things to do to make a business thrive and fly. Resting into a developmental model means you don't have to be doing the equivalent of trying to teach a toddler to walk, read, drive, and hold down a job all at the same time, especially when it doesn't yet have the ability to do most of those things.

Chapters 6 and 7 are explicitly about marketing. While marketing is not the only thing a business needs, it is consistently the most challenging part of making a microbusiness work. We have a long history at Heart of Business of helping people who come in hating marketing, then learn to love it, because they learn that marketing is something very different than what they thought.

These chapters teach the true purpose of marketing, which is NOT attraction. They also bring in the Three Journeys of Marketing so you can let go of the lie that you need to somehow convert absolute strangers into instant buyers. That lie is the source of much pain, manipulation, and toxicity in the world of business.

Chapter 8 explains the five success qualities. I delve into the top five heart qualities that I've seen most consistently in people who are successful with their businesses. It's a little different than you might have seen before in the business world and does not include "courage" or "willingness to take risks."

Chapter 9 delineates the ten necessary, practical elements for your business. These elements can't really be skipped; if you miss one, your business will limp along. They are further detailed and expanded in a one-hundred-plus-item checklist we placed in the appendix. You can see the practical roadmap of what parts you need to put in place over several years, to help your business thrive. Although some people feel overwhelmed at first, most end up feeling a deep sense of compassion for themselves once they understand the scale of what they're working on and why it's okay that it takes a few years to build up.

Chapters 10 and 11 get you on the path. Now that you are in the process of healing your relationship with business and money, and you have a developmental understanding of business as well as a heart-centered approach to marketing, these two chapters give you sustenance for the path forward. Chapter 10 is about letting go of toxic beliefs about what it takes to succeed, deeply listening to your own business, then identifying the true commitment that is being asked of you. Hint: it's not working twenty-four seven every day of the year.

Chapter 11 is about embracing the journey. It helps you integrate the content of the book, and it also helps to break myths about productivity: about what counts as "work" and why most people vastly underestimate what they can get done. It helps you identify what you need moving forward and how to get your arms around what's involved.

Along the way, you'll see links and QR codes that lead you to supporting material. Often the exercises in this book are easier if you are guided into them; we created easy access so you can relax into the journey.

A Little About Mark

My first taste of business was around 1979, when I joined a chapter of Junior Achievement in junior high school, where young people supposedly learn about business. Usually, kids make coffee mug holders and try to sell them to understand how business works. Instead, I had the bright idea of going to organizations, asking them to buy t-shirts, and taking their orders to a t-shirt making company that made the t-shirts.

We made a profit just by being in the middle of the transaction, and we outperformed all the JA chapters for hundreds of miles by 1000 percent. I received a check for around $100, which in 1979 was a big deal to eleven-year-old me. My conclusion? We were a scam, the business was unethical, we weren't actually doing any work. I don't know if I'd completely agree today; there was some work involved, after all. But that understanding helped me see through so much crap going on in the business world all around me. It began an education on how corporations and the money they brought to the political process corrupted our public institutions.

A few years after that, I got into the Washington, DC, punk-rock scene and started protesting the US government and large corporations. Forty years later, I think my parents are beginning to suspect this isn't a phase I'm going to grow out of.

Speaking of family, I grew up in small business. My grandfather, my mother's father, an Orthodox Jew who immigrated from Russia in the early 1900s, became a pharmacist. In the 1930s, during Prohibition when alcohol was illegal here in the US, he sold alcohol by prescription in his pharmacy. When Prohibition ended, he opened a wine and liquor store where he worked well into his nineties. My parents took it over from him, and I grew up with the store a central part of my family life.

After years of activism, including abortion rights/clinic defense, coming out as bisexual in 1988, queer activism, and eventually running a nonprofit magazine as a volunteer while working as a paramedic in the San Francisco Bay Area, I began to feel burned out. Burned out on the anger. Burned out on always being in reaction to negative events. And burned out on the violence, racism, food deserts, poverty, and hopelessness I saw while running 911 calls in Vallejo, then Oakland, California.

My wife, Holly Glaser, whom I met in 1994, was much more aware of the spiritual side of things than I was. Before we met, she had also been an activist who was going to be an environmental rights lawyer, but because of a head injury in a car accident, her sharp analytic mind was replaced by a growing awareness of her intuitive, heart-based gifts, which she was deepening and growing into when we met.

I tell you this because when I was burned out and thinking about what else I could do, I ended up helping a few self-employed friends by creating marketing materials for them. I had some of those skills from my time running the magazine, and they were doing things like selling handmade soaps and lotions or helping people with backyard organic gardening. Holly, herself, was building a massage and healing practice.

I was a terrible graphic designer, but to my surprise I knew a lot more about marketing and being in business than I had realized. And I felt great about supporting my friends with small businesses to do fantastic work in the world.

But these friends had so much emotional struggle over things like pricing, marketing, and just being in business in general. I said to Holly, "I really need to know how to help people process emotionally. What do I need to learn?"

That's when Holly introduced me to Sufi spiritual healing, which she had just discovered herself. We became students of a Sufi sheikh, Muhammad Sa'id al-Jamal ar-Rifa'i as-Shadhuli, one of the main teachers at the Al-Aqsa Mosque in Jerusalem, one of Islam's three holiest sites. Sidi, as he was known to his thousands of students around the globe, was head of the Higher Sufi council in Jerusalem. He taught the primacy of love and mercy, justice and freedom, through Sufism, the mystical teachings of Islam.

Several things happened to me as a Sufi student. One is that I learned how to access love in my heart: consistently, powerfully, and in surprising ways. Sufism is, as many spiritual paths are, a path of surrender, devotion, humility, and service, and that nourished me deeply.

Learning those teachings also helped me become a healer and a teacher in the way of the love.

The other thing that happened for me that I'll mention here is that I was shown in my heart how business practices and esoteric spiritual teachings overlay each other: how certain business practices mirror deeper spiritual teachings. This had a profound effect on me because instead of "spirituality in business" meaning fill up your personal gas tank with spirituality then use it up while doing business, I found that the doing of business could itself be a spiritual practice, that we could be nourished in the doing of it.

As I began to integrate the business knowledge I had and continued to learn with the Sufi teachings, Heart of Business was born. Since then, and especially since earning my Master of Divinity, I've been honored to speak with people from many, many different spiritual paths and religions. I have found what so many others before me have found: that we're all touching on a universal truth—just talking about and accessing it in different ways.

Heart of Business was born in 2001, and since that time I—and Holly, who mentored and supported me into teaching—have worked with over four thousand different business owners and aspiring business owners. We help them to integrate love and business development, and we support them in holding their commitments to integrity, justice, care, and service while also thriving in this dysfunctional economy.

This book holds more than two decades of experience and wisdom. My hope for you is that it nourishes your heart as well as guides your strategy as you go about the beautiful work of developing your business.

> *When you find the love, you find yourself. The secret is in the love. You are the love, not another. Everything is in the love, and everyone needs the love. If you find this, what more could you want? When you know, what could you want? When you have the knowledge of the love, you feel peace in your heart. The jewels are inside you.*
>
> —Sufi Sheikh Sidi Muhammad al-Jamal, from his book *Music of the Soul.*

CHAPTER 1

Healing Your Relationship with Business

If you have any negative feelings about business, you should. I do not want you to "get over" them. Your upset is justified.

I had a client who consulted and trained for large corporations. A portion of the work they did was helping folks in those companies see more deeply into their own hearts, their needs, their lives. They held that thriving professionally meant discovering what was true at their center: what was most in alignment and integrity for them.

As a result, a certain percentage of their clients discovered that when looked at honestly, their hearts and integrity couldn't support the work they did. Many of them left their careers to pursue lives that allowed them to sleep peacefully.

This is not an uncommon story. It's all too common.

Anyone with a heart would have legitimate, painful reactions to business in this world. For hundreds of years, during the era of modern capitalism, the way humans have done business has been increasingly terrible.

Shortsighted, greedy, and, in some cases, downright evil, human beings have made business decisions that have ravaged the environment; undermined and destroyed cultures; killed countless people; and resulted in global recessions. All in the name of profit. On a large scale, we've all watched the various petroleum companies fund climate-change-denying "science" and lobby hard against environmental regulation or controls, despite the cliff's edge we're hurtling toward as a planet.

Plus, as documented heavily in books like *The Half Has Never Been Told*, by Cornell University professor of history Edward Baptist, the wealth of the United States in particular, and much of the western world in general, was generated through the horrific practices of chattel slavery and white supremacy.

Currently, prisoners in the United States generate an estimated eleven billion dollars annually in goods and services, some of it for private corporations, while being paid at most fifty cents per hour—but often much less or nothing.

The 2008 recession that rocked housing markets and general economies across the globe was sparked because of unethical, unregulated practices in the financial industry. Monstrous profits were pocketed, while millions of regular people were left in dire situations.

In the decades prior, many of us watched big-box stores underprice and undermine local, family-owned businesses in small towns everywhere. Then we watched that same dynamic play out on the internet. Big companies still report record profits; owners and executives stash millions, even billions, in personal wealth. All while most of us struggle even to make ends meet, many relying on minimal government assistance to get by.

Ugh. These are some of the more extreme injustices that have become commonplace within our economy. We could spend the rest of the book just listing the damaging excesses and harmful results of the traumatic and traumatizing economy we live in.

It's not so surprising that my client's clients and many others like them chose to leave or make other significant changes when their hearts awakened to the reality they were, often unconsciously, helping to prop up.

The demands of business within the relatively recently invented ideology of capitalism have made many of us deeply unhappy, mentally unwell, and physically sick.

Healing business—doing business from the heart—can never be the entire solution to these problems. So much of the healing is in reclaiming parts of our culture as public and as personal—not to be reduced to transactions or measured for profitability.

But heart-centered business is a necessary and impactful part of the healing. Doing business in a heart-centered way is needed to shift the economy and to heal our cultures and ourselves.

For us—you and me—healing our relationship with business is not a process of putting on rose-colored glasses, accepting the evils, smiling and looking away, or simply "getting over it." Healing is a way to come into wholeness.

The path to wholeness includes grief about what is and what has been. It's also an embrace of what's possible. As

MARK SILVER ✧ HEART CENTERED BUSINESS

I sometimes say, it's equal parts gentleness and boldness. When we grieve, we honor the painful parts of the truth, and we make it possible to begin to set things right.

But before you can heal your relationship with business in general and *your business* in particular, we need to answer the question *What IS business?* We do business, we're in business, we work with businesses. But what is the thing itself?

The Essence of Business

When I've asked people in workshops "What's the essence of business?," I've received a variety of answers. Most folks offer a version of: "Business is about transacting services or goods for money."

That's part of what one *does* in business. But any transaction that occurs is not the essence of business.

So then we start to look at the things involved in the business: those things that make up the transaction process. Things like clients, customers, workers, owners, equipment, computers, apps, services, products, money, paperwork, colleagues, corporate entities, government regulating agencies—you get the point.

Those things are the elements involved in getting business done. But it's obvious that none of them encompass business's essence, either. And none of them are universal to every business—except people, and maybe money.

I want to offer an understanding of business that I came to after wrestling with all this over the course of many years:

The essence of business doesn't lie in the things transacted, nor the elements of transaction, nor the individuals

involved in transacting. The heart of business, rather, lies in the aliveness of the so-called "space between." It's *dynamic relationships*, not particular things and persons and systems and structures, that constitute the essence of business.

The things transacted, the elements of transaction, and the individuals involved in transaction comprise merely the actions of business, not its essence. The heart of business, the essence of its aliveness, is in the relationships between all these things. Many have said that business is about relationships, but they usually only mean relationships between people.

I'm saying that the essence of business is not a *thing*; it's the dynamic aliveness in the relationships between anything and anyone having to do with one's livelihood.

This relational understanding is more profound than it might appear at first, and it disrupts some of the business-as-usual practices and beliefs.

Things like:

- **The "It's Not Personal" myth:** This myth says that business is somehow not personal, that we shouldn't, can't, have enduring relationships of warmth and care within the context of business. This is not true. We can and should have relationships of warmth and care in whatever context we find ourselves. There is no realm of human life exempted from the presence of love and care.

- **The "Be Professional" myth:** Being professional has come to mean being cold, distant, and impersonal, with a veneer of insincere politeness. That's not professional; that's inhuman. Professional instead means doing your best to be of service, while being in a sincere, authentic relationship with the folks around you.

- **The "Profit Reigns Supreme" myth:** This myth says that the highest priority is making as much money as possible. While a healthy business does well financially, short-term profit at the cost of relationships is damaging to the long-term viability of the business. This most obviously references relationships with clients, employees, or customers. But it also includes relationships with the tools of our trades, with the communities our businesses are in, and with the planet.

When we see the business in terms of relationships, it's easy to see that damaging a relationship damages the business.

Does this mean we tolerate all relationships, including toxic ones? No, it means that healthy businesses are constituted by healthy relationships.

My grandfather, who was an orthodox Jewish immigrant from Russia in the early 1900s, had a retail store in Washington, DC that my parents eventually ran. They ran a healthy business on the basis of healthy relationships with the local community and their employees and customers. But they also did not live by the myth, "The Customer is Always Right."

My mom likes to tell the story of someone who came into the store and made a racist comment to one of the employees. She stepped up to this customer and told them immediately that they weren't welcome in the store. The business lost a customer, but the relationship with that customer could never have been healthy without that customer healing and transforming the white supremacy they carried. It would have been damaging to the humanity of everyone, especially the employees who were the targets of this person's racism.

I think it's important to mention here that, as my friend and colleague Desiree Adaway of the Adaway Group always says, we get free together. Compassion and love are so important on the path of justice. Undoing systems of oppression—including white supremacy, predatory capitalism, and patriarchy, that have so distorted all our relationships—requires every single one of us. If you want, as I do, a truly healthy society where we all are included, valued, and celebrated, we all need to learn how to create healthy relationships in every aspect of our life. Business is not separate from this.

In my learning and growth here, I need to acknowledge many people who have helped me in big ways: in particular Desiree, as well as Nicole Lee of Inclusive Life and Lani Ka'ahumanu, my first mentor in activism.

Healthy businesses *necessitate* healthy relationships. Tolerating unhealthy relationships is not healthy for the business, nor for you.

Moving toward Health

You might be thinking: if healthy business is about healthy relationships, then my ship is sunk, because I feel totally overwhelmed trying to manage all the relationships that constitute my business! I've got relationships with:

- Past clients/customers
- Current clients/customers
- Future clients/customers
- Employees or other team members
- Competitors
- Web developers
- Other businesses of which my business is a customer
- Accountants

And the list goes on and on!

Of course, managing all those relationships individually can swiftly become overwhelming. This is especially true because thriving businesses tend to have relationships with many more people than an individual would ordinarily have in a community. A successful practice may have relationships with an audience of 500 to 1500, or even more, while an individual might have fifty to 150 people in their personal circle.

And it's more relationships than just people. Yesterday I dropped my laptop. Actually, I'd forgotten to tighten the knob on my laptop stand, so it just flopped over, sending my laptop to the floor. So now I'm writing this on my iPad.

I'm saying this because we also have relationships with things. Our devices. Our office space. Government agencies like the Internal Revenue Service, the tax collector here in the US. Plus all the services one uses.

It's *a lot* with which to be in conscious relationship. Systems and team obviously play a role in reducing the overwhelm, and we get to those topics later in this book. But they don't entirely solve the problem.

To solve this kind of relational overwhelm and move toward health for your business will require a leap more fundamental and essential.

Spirituality in Business

Spirituality can be a touchy subject for many, so I'll start with what I *don't* mean by this word.

Spirituality is not a bearded guy in the sky judging us and telling us what to do. It's not a list of rules that you must follow or be cast away. It's not anything external to us.

My upbringing is Jewish, and my spiritual path for more than two decades is Islamic Sufism. The teachings are profound in that they bring an immersive recipe of surrender, sincerity, and devotion that melt the barriers of perception to witnessing the presence of the Divine Love in everything.

For me, that was the most self-opening and heart-opening realization. Love, the Divine, the Mystery, doesn't have to be invited in or even brought into any place. It's up to us, the human, to work to perceive that love is already present in everything.

It's true that human intention can distort and veil the experience of love in so many things. But the essential nature of anything that exists is love. Everything comes from love, and everything returns to love; there is nothing that is outside the love.

This means that the long list of people and things we are in relationship with through business is really just one relationship: our relationship with the Source of Love.

Your client is an expression of the Source of Love. Your colleague is also an expression of that same Source. Your web designer, your laptop, your money—all the things, and your business itself, are expressions of the Source.

I do not mean this glibly, and this is not an excuse to tolerate difficulties and injustices "because it's all from love."

It has to do with *how* we are in relationship to the many things and people in the world around us. It would be false to conclude that because everything is, in its essence, Divine, then this must mean everything is okay. This toxic teaching gets used to excuse so many harms perpetrated on others. "Love and light!" are showered around instead of working to quench our implacable thirst for justice and care.

But this notion that all things somehow belong to the Source of Love *is* relevant to how we engage. This Divine truth speaks to what we know of the natural world: that nothing can be thrown out because there is no "out." No one and no thing can be discarded because we are all real expressions of the Oneness. It all belongs. We all belong.

When we cannot make the easy judgment to get rid of things, then we must face the aliveness of discovering a healthy relationship with all. Sometimes that means the healthy relationship is a very distant relationship. Or it means that work is involved in making the relationship healthy.

This applies in so many ways to aspects of your business. Hate marketing? It can't be discarded, but it also doesn't have to be dealt with as an evil, monstrous, terrible thing. You can find the love within it and engage in a healthy relationship with it. Many clients in our Heart of Business Community have learned to love marketing—not by trampling their values, but by embracing marketing's deeper essence. We'll be getting into this in a later chapter.

The question, then, is: How do we remember love, especially in facing a difficult situation in business—whether it's racism or sexism, overwork and overwhelm, marketing or another task we don't like, or any other toxic relational dynamic?

Healing through Remembrance

To answer that, I want to introduce you to a simple Sufi practice called Remembrance. This practice is not specific to any religion, and I didn't invent it. It's been taught to truly countless spiritual students over the centuries, and I myself have successfully taught it to thousands of entrepreneurs of all spiritual paths.

I'll say here that in the Qur'an, the holy book from which I most frequently study, it says very clearly, "There is no compulsion in religion." [Q: 2:256] It also says very clearly, "We have created you ... and made you peoples and tribes, so that you might come to know one another." [Q: 49:13] For me, this means that we each walk the path of the Divine in different ways according to where our heart places us. My most sincere intention is that whatever I share from my particular path and lineage helps you to deepen in your own path, whatever that is.

What I share of the Sufi teachings is given as a gift, and I hope that you find it nourishing in your own spiritual journey.

So, exactly what *is* Remembrance?

Like most spiritual practices, the Remembrance is deceptively simple. To "do" Remembrance, or to "be in" Remembrance, one calls the/a name of the Divine into the heart. For example, one simply says, inwardly or outwardly: "Mystery," or "God," or "Universe," or "Allah," or "One," or "Nature," or any other term denoting divinity.

Right away, difficulties arise.

First of all: a name? Call a name? Call *the* name? Why use a name at all? Isn't that limiting the awareness of the Infinite?

Sufism finds that calling a name is extremely useful, for a few different reasons. For one, we're practicing being in relationship with the Divine, whom the Sufis sometimes refer to as the Beloved. To be in relationship with someone or something means that someone or something has a name.

I personally don't find names limiting—unless you mean a *label* and not a name. My wife Holly and I have been together since 1994, twenty-eight years as I'm writing this. Even after all that time, we continue to surprise each other and grow. Yet her name hasn't changed since I met her. Her name doesn't limit her, and my name doesn't limit me. A name is a doorway to the reality of who, Who, this person is before you.

The calling of the name is one that arises from devotion, from yearning. When speaking of spiritual practices, there are, broadly speaking, *devotional practices* and *contemplative practices*. Both are important, and many paths include both kinds. A *contemplative practice* is often, but not always, a practice of emptying out. Of letting go, detaching. Many forms of meditation are contemplative, with the intention that in letting go of attachments, we make way for a much larger reality to take root in one's awareness.

Devotional practices lean into the natural tendency of the heart to attach. Using the power of love, one turns one's devotion, one's yearning, toward something. For Sufis, whose practices often emphasize the devotional more than the contemplative, we turn our yearning toward the Oneness, the Beloved, the Divine Source of Love. This has the same ultimate goal as contemplative practices, through the intention of attaching to the Most High, which subsumes all other attachments.

Connecting to love, however one does that, is central to heart-centered business practices. There are many times in the context of business when we are urged to overlook love, care, or other fundamental values. Having a way to connect amid the overwhelm, the whirl, the pressure, is so important. One reason I love the Remembrance is because, as a practice, it is simple and available in every moment. A practice like this, calling a name in your heart, can happen in a breath, changing everything in a moment.

Another question, among many, is *which name*? I have two somewhat contradictory thoughts about this. As in many spiritual realities, there's a tension between two extremes that helps us find something real.

The first thought is that you want a name that feels comfortable to your heart and points you toward the highest reality possible. A name that opens your heart and calls to a reality beyond our limitations. So many people have been injured by mishandled spiritual and religious teachings, sometimes deliberately. The trauma is real, the pain is to be honored, and using a name that retriggers those experiences is often quite unhelpful.

The second thought, which creates a tension with the first, is that you shouldn't work too hard to find a name perfect for you. The truth is, when we meet someone, we don't get to pick their name. When I met Holly and she told me her name, I didn't get to say, "Well, that doesn't quite suit me, I need a different name for you." Many names of the Divine, despite how they've been misused, are older than the abuse. They are sacred in their essence. We don't want abusers to lay sole claim to names that have held a profound reality for generations.

For myself, I use the Divine name "Allah." It means "The One" or "the God." It's beyond form, beyond male or female. It has that lovely "aaahhhh" sound, twice, that resonates deeply in the heart. And it is ancient. The holy teacher Jesus, in his native language of Aramaic, used the Divine name "Alaha," which is very much related to Allah.

I had my issues with the name Allah, as someone raised Jewish in the United States. But I've found that for me it is a deeply resonant way of connecting through my heart.

In the practice I'm about to describe, try a few different names if you aren't already settled on one. Notice how they feel in your heart. And, all the while, bear in mind that this is about nurturing a relationship with a sacred Source: a relationship that will open avenues for healing and growth within you, your business, and beyond.

The Practice of Remembrance

By nature, it's challenging to teach a spiritual practice in written form. If you'd like to listen to a short audio of me teaching the Remembrance, you can find it here:

www.heartcenteredbusinessbook/resources/remembrance

However, if you would like to try here and now, the practice is straightforward.

You call the Name, a name, of the Divine into your heart.

This is not a mechanical action. It's not, "Do this, then that happens." It's a relationship. It's a name of the Beloved. You are calling to the Beloved within the depths of your heart.

And then you're listening for the response.

And then you call again.

The calling is something that arises from an original yearning within us. In Islam, *hadith* are sayings of the Prophet

Muhammad, peace be upon him and upon all prophets. A special type of hadith, the *hadith qudsi*, are considered direct quotes from God. One of the most famous is this one. "I was a hidden treasure and I yearned to be known. So I created the creation in order to be known."

The Sufis consider this original yearning to be known the Divine spark that lives in each of our hearts. The calling, the Remembrance, is exactly that. A profound, unquenchable yearning rising up and calling out: "Allah! Allah! Allah!"

When I do the Remembrance, am in the Remembrance, when I'm Remembering, I often start first with noticing how I feel and what's true for me in the moment.

Then, as I begin to call to the Beloved within my heart—and this is one of the most important points—I don't try to fix or change how I'm feeling. The calling can sometimes sound like: "Is love available even here? Is the Divine present even here?" And the "here" may mean frustrated, angry, bored, overwhelmed, disconnected, numb—whatever is true in the moment (whether business-related or otherwise).

Many of us get caught in the picture that spiritual practice means we're supposed to feel peaceful or full of love, and that if we don't, we should be trying to reach that state.

I've never found that to be helpful or effective. Of course we yearn for the love. But rather than try to force myself into that state of feeling the intimacy, I find sincerity more nourishing for my heart. For example: "I'm so alone and overwhelmed, and I'm yearning for the love and don't feel it. Allah!"

And then listening, noticing, perceiving. Then again.

It's not uncommon for folks to feel nothing, or very little, in the Remembrance. There are many reasons for that. Here are the two most common.

☼

Trauma Blocks Connection

So many of us have had significant emotional, spiritual, physical, or sexual trauma, that there's a numbness or distance inside. If you have trauma reactions, spiritual practice alone will usually be insufficient to bring full healing. I highly recommend you work with an experienced, compassionate trauma therapist, one who works somatically, with the body, to release the trauma from your nervous system.

I had mild Post-Traumatic Stress Disorder (PTSD) from my time as a paramedic in Oakland, California. I would get flashback memories and an ongoing constant vigilance in my nervous system that exhausted me and made it very difficult to be aware of the subtle inside my heart. I had some sessions with a somatic therapist to release the trauma in my body. Afterward, spiritual connection was much easier for me.

There's another reason for not feeling much.

Called to Subtlety

Being in our physical lives, we're used to very dramatic sensations coming in. Spiritual practice, heart connection, asks us to be aware, to perceive on a much more subtle level.

I was guiding a client into Remembrance, and they told me they felt "nothing." I asked them, "How do you know you feel nothing? What does nothing feel like?" They brought their attention to the numbness in their heart, and after some moments, began to describe it like this: "My heart feels stiff, cold, a bit distant." I encouraged them to stay with that perception as they continued to call the Name into their heart, taking care not to try to change or fix the stiffness or coldness.

As they continued to call the Name of their choice into their heart, taking their time, finding patience and persistence and gentleness, along with a willingness to just be with the stiffness and cold, they started to report a slight warmth: a "melting" in the heart.

For me, at the same time, before they spoke, I could feel a slightly more warmth in the room. I noticed that their face looked more relaxed and there was more of a glow, if you will, about them.

As they continued their work with me, with the Remembrance, with a willingness to be aware of the subtle and trust their heart, they found that the practice came alive for them. Not always very dramatically, but they found a reliable way to connect with their heart, however their heart was in that moment.

I'm saying "call to subtlety," but after a while, it's not really that subtle. It's just been outside our awareness. The metaphor I sometimes use is a movie theater. If you sit in the front row, with the screen taking up most of your awareness, the sights and sounds of the movie can overwhelm your perceptions. You think the movie is all that's going on. For some people, this can be a fun way to watch a movie. But it's not a very effective way to live life.

The Remembrance enables you to move toward the back of the theater, where you can still stay engaged with the story of your life, yet you realize that the screen is flat and there's a much larger reality containing your story. You notice that there are other seats, other people, and even an Exit to a larger world.

The Remembrance is simply that: a remembering that there is a larger reality around us, a presence available in every moment. We forget, then we Remember, then we forget, then we Remember again.

The more we practice Remembering, the easier it is to witness and experience the larger reality all around.

Back to Healing Your Relationship with Business

Healing is in the details. I've become convinced that attempting to heal a pattern in one's life or business can be a big block to finding true healing. Instead, if we bring healing to the small details or moments, that focused healing loosens the dysfunction of the larger patterns, eventually allowing large shifts to happen.

We often have a distant, intellectual understanding of the larger pattern. That lack of vulnerability and intimacy with the pattern is what keeps us distant from the healing as well. Yet we often have a very up-close and personal relationship with the details.

If you're trying to heal your relationship with business, start by looking at some aspect of business that sparks anxiety or upset in you. For instance, many business owners feel negativity about the sales conversation. Try leaning into the discomfort around that conversation. Try bringing the Remembrance to it. Ask in your heart, "Is love available even here?" and just allow yourself to be with the discomfort, the reactions, and the love. In so doing, you might experience that subtle "heart melting" I mentioned above.

From this sitting and being with, two things often emerge. First: you find it's not fatal to be with the discomfort of the sales conversation. You might discover you can face it.

Second: in seeing it, in coming into a more intimate relationship with it, you can begin to discern what parts feel fine, and what parts give rise to discomfort. Then you can begin to work with those parts to transform them until the entire process feels whole, healed, perhaps even sacred.

Sometimes this healing can be done alone, with just your own internal resources. Other times, you might discover the need for an outside source that can bring information, encouragement, guidance, and nourishment to your heart as it seeks new ways of understanding. For instance, we've put a heart-centered frame around sales and other aspects of business that helps our clients step toward those pieces of building their businesses much more easily.

Even with a new frame this process is made more effective when there is a specific situation at hand. So instead of trying to heal your relationship with sales conversations, there may have been a *particular* sales conversation, perhaps with a potential client or seller, which elicited a negative and uncomfortable reaction inside you. By being with the details of that specific conversation, the "off" parts are more easily and concretely identified. The way is now opened to a deeper healing—one that can subsequently be applied to other situations.

An example may help. We had a member of our community who had struggled with the sales conversation. For this person, all the Remembrance and healing on the topic of sales didn't really move the dial.

What *did* move the dial, what *did* open her heart and enable her to engage, was to focus on a specific instance: how intimidated she felt talking to a particular potential client. In Remembrance, she saw how she imagined that they were critical of her and that they didn't really want the help. In a process of staying present to all that arose for her as she faced the idea of being in a sales conversation with that potential client, a lot of what had been wrapped around it became clear to her: so much of her own fear, shame, and vulnerability.

She was, in time, able to see that this person was not critical of her, just nervous and vulnerable about getting help. Standing in a healthy framework for heart-centered sales, seeing a deeper truth in her own heart about what was actually going on, she could breathe again.

This healed her relationship with that sales conversation. It also helped to heal her relationship with so much about sales in general.

And it was a pivotal healing for her in her relationship with marketing, too. She suddenly saw that marketing for her could just be about getting help to people who needed it. *So* much shifted!

This shift occurred because she started with the details, with a single conversation. Had she tried to heal "selling" at a theoretical, intellectual level, the dial would not have moved.

Reading the example above may or may not have catalyzed any healing for you. Perhaps it resonated somewhat or sparked something inside. Maybe you understood it intellectually but couldn't connect personally to the experience. This is perfectly understandable, and it's what I want to emphasize. Our client didn't get healing because she conceptualized it in her mind. The healing happened because she experienced it in her heart—profoundly. This transformative experience then gave rise to her renewed understanding.

Healing your own relationship with business will most likely unfold the same way. When you bring your attention to some painful aspect of being in business, then use love and Remembrance to untangle that particular knot, you open the doorway to healing. It becomes even easier when you have a new, heart-centered frame with which to understand some aspect of business, as our client did with our approach to selling.

When we look at all the many knotted places, attending to the details can seem like a slow, painstaking, and painful way to go. Surprisingly, however, it's the swiftest and most efficient way forward. Unraveling a single knot loosens other knots. What our clients discover is that they don't have to unravel every single knot. Instead, knot by knot, they will reach a point when the whole tapestry suddenly unravels. The mess of threads can then be rewoven with love, in a much healthier way.

Untangling One Knot

For this exercise, especially the first time you do it, I recommend picking a topic or challenge that isn't something that has been a huge block for you. Start with something smaller so you can get your heart around the exercise without confronting the biggest knot you're facing in business.

Plus, remember that by untangling a few knots, you can loosen the whole structure of stuckness.

If you want to be led through this exercise, there is short audio you can listen to here.

www.heartcenteredbusinessbook.com/resources/one-knot

1. **Start by picking an area in business—something specific—where you feel stuck, resistant, upset, or avoidant in some way.** Pick something as specific as possible. If you start with a broad area, like money

or charging money, focus in to pick something like, "Charging enough money for my individual sessions."

Example: I feel so tangled up about marketing, but I get that that's too big and broad. So I'll focus in on one thing in marketing, I'll pick how stuck and shy I feel thinking about asking one of my favorite clients to send me referrals.

2. **As you think of this thing that you're stuck around, let yourself feel the reactions that rise in you.** Fear, sadness, anger, grief? Whatever is there, and whatever thoughts arise, there is room for that. Take a breath and be with what arises without trying to fix or change anything.

Example: When I think about asking him to send me referrals, I feel so frozen and scared. I'm worried about doing it wrong, I'm worried about upsetting him, maybe losing him as a client. My shoulders, my throat, my belly are all really tight, and I'm having trouble taking a deep breath. Ugh!

3. **Start to practice the Remembrance, calling a name of the Divine through the open doorway of your heart.** Do it without trying to fix or change anything, without trying to relax or make it better. It's as if you're asking, "Is there love even here? Is the Divine present, even here, in the struggle, in the knot?"

Example: It took a lot of effort to bring my attention back to my heart and to start the Remembrance. As I did, I felt silly, but I let myself continue to ask, "Is love available even here? Is the Divine even here?" As I did so, I felt a slight warmth in my chest. I felt my belly start to relax. I felt myself able to take a breath.

4. **From Remembrance, bring the questions: "What deeper truth am I not seeing about this situation? What is here that my heart wants to show me?"** Allow yourself to ask it in a way that lets you sit back, that avoids reaching for answers and instead opens to curiosity and wondering. Bring a willingness to be surprised.

   Example: It took a while to further settle down, although it helped to already be doing the Remembrance. I really wanted to see or hear something from my heart, but gradually I let go of that, too, just wondering what's here, what my heart wants to show me. I felt like I finally let go of my worry that my client wouldn't like me, and I could just be willing to be surprised. As I did, I felt a silence in my heart and a deeper sense of trust and relaxation. I heard something like, "He already likes and trusts you. He would be delighted to support you, to support others getting help from you. It's no burden to him at all." As I heard this message, I realized how true it felt and my whole being relaxed. I also remembered that I'm reading this book and there might be information in it about asking for referrals. I realized I could let myself finish the book before trying anything challenging. So much relief. The knot definitely feels much looser.

This exercise is fairly straightforward and simple. The examples are ones I've seen happen with clients. Not everyone gets that kind of clarity straight off. Sometimes folks just get a slight bit of loosening, easing the ability to breathe, and that's enough to take the next step.

There's so much about the world of business that is all knotted up in us. Loosening just one knot at a time can help to open a new path for you.

✿

Things to Remember

- You don't need to get over your issues with business. Anyone with a heart would have issues with business. The way business has been distorted over the last two to three centuries is deeply disturbing.
- Everything comes from love, ultimately. While it has been distorted and veiled in nearly all aspects of business, you can discover the love within everything.
- The essence of business is relationship, and it's our relationships with everyone and everything in and around our business. Healthy relationships equal healthy business.
- Having a healthy relationship with your business is foundational to healing both your business and business in general.
- Healing is in the details. Start with small, individual "knots." As these untangle, more will be transformed.

With this foundational learning in place, let's dive into the next topic: money!

CHAPTER 2

Healing Your Relationship with Money

Just as I don't want you to minimize your discomforts with business, I do *not* want you to "get over" your issues with money. If you struggle with money, if you have reactions to money, they are coming—at least in part—from wisdom.

Money has been used in terrible ways to support injustice, to keep people from having enough, and to create competition where none need exist. Larger corporations often operate with profit as their sole aim, regardless of the destruction wrought. Fights over money have torn families apart and are the cause of many wars.

Money is distributed unjustly, too. Jobs that have to do with caring for people often pay poverty-level wages, whereas jobs centered on further manipulating the financial and business markets are the highest paid.

So if you have negative reactions to money, those reactions exist for very good, legitimate reasons.

That said, continuing the theme of the previous chapter, there is a way for you to engage with money without collapsing, turning away, or going into fight mode. We're in a world where money exists, and you and your business need to deal with it.

Since 2002, I have taught an entire course on having a healthier relationship with money: The Heart of Money and Power Transformational Journey. In what follows, I will invite you toward some core inner shifts. These shifts will not only begin to heal your relationship with money but will also support you in creating a heart-centered business. More broadly, you may even find them helpful for living a life more deeply rooted in wisdom and love.

If it seems like there is some repetition in the teachings and practices I recommend, there is. You'll notice that throughout the book I bring the same or similar fundamental teachings and exercises into new contexts, which should strengthen your ability to learn and apply them throughout different areas of your business.

Pennies from Heaven Miracles versus Workaday Miracles

Many people who want healing with money are looking for, or maybe are taught to expect, what I've come to call the "Pennies from Heaven" miracle. The miracle happens: you suddenly receive a windfall of money from an unexpected source. A tax refund, or an inheritance from a distant relative, or a debt someone owed you that you forgot about, or, of course, the proverbial lottery ticket. The money just comes gushing in.

This happens, obviously. People experience this. However, miracles like this are not the focus of this book. As a Sufi teacher, I'm not in the business of trying to control the Divine, like turning on a water faucet.

Instead, I find it far more effective to focus on what I call "workaday" miracles. These are indeed miracles, but they are miracles that arise out of a changed relationship, a clearer perception.

For instance, you may have associations with debt that leave you feeling powerless, collapsed, and ashamed. So you struggle to pay your debts.

In this instance, healing comes as you turn unflinching eyes toward your relationship with a *particular* debt. Can you invite the Divine there? Can you ask, gently, "Is love available even here?" As you engage some of the approaches we teach, your heart begins to see this debt—and debt in general—very differently.

That difference can leave you feeling lighter, more empowered, more at ease. Instead of feeling collapsed around the debt, you begin to see actions you can take. Maybe you reach out to a debt counselor who helps you negotiate a smaller debt and easier terms. Perhaps your heart shifts in such a way that you don't feel like you have to throw every last penny at the debt. Instead, you pay a reasonable amount toward it (even if it's less than they are asking) and retain some in savings so you can build reserves up gradually, without anxiety or shame.

Perhaps you see that the expenses of your life in general are more than you were previously able to face. But in seeing it, you feel a sense of empowerment around raising the prices in your business. Suddenly your income jumps by 15 to 20 percent, and it's all much easier.

These are workaday miracles.

I'm thinking of a client we helped who did several of these things: they faced their debt, took stock of their household budget, and raised their prices by 15 percent. This added hundreds of dollars into their monthly revenue. So much ease resulted.

Consider the implications of raising your rates 15 percent. If you normally charge $75 per session and have fifteen sessions per month, that's $1,125 in income. But if you charge $86 per session, which is a 15-percent raise, and still have fifteen sessions, your income jumps to $1,290—a $165 monthly raise. Then maybe you decide to raise prices a bit more, and you learn how to effectively and comfortably invite clients to get the additional sessions they need, maybe two per month instead of one, or four instead of two, and you jump to having twenty sessions. Twenty sessions at $95 each is not a big leap in real-world terms. But suddenly you find you're making $775 more per month.

To make this real, a client of mine who was exhausted and wanted to shift to a more sustainable business model realized she could raise her prices 15 to 20 percent and bring in $1,000 more per month without any additional work. What's more, she saw that she hadn't raised her prices in several years, and it was long overdue.

These kinds of shifts can feel incredibly emotionally significant. But businesswise, they're relatively small, even as they can have a huge impact on your sustainability. That's what I mean by workaday miracles.

In this chapter, I want to introduce several core teachings and offer one fundamental exercise that will help you begin to heal your relationship with money.

Money Is Physical

If you've moved in spiritual circles you might have heard things like "money is energy." I want to contradict that. Money is not energy. Money only exists as money, with purchasing power and all, on the physical plane.

Thinking about money as energy can, in fact, feed into financial problems. When money is spiritualized, that obscures the fact that it is a physical tool with specific uses in the real world.

From a Sufi point of view, it's true that everything is ultimately Divine. The Sufis understand the world and the things in it as expressions of Divine qualities. These Divine qualities are things like Love, Strength, Wisdom, Compassion, Mercy, and Freedom. There are ninety-nine of these qualities in the Sufi tradition. I see parallels to this understanding in other traditions. Judaism, for instance, has the seventy-two names of the Divine, which is directly equivalent to the Sufi Divine names. Hinduism has many different gods, yet still a belief in Oneness. The various gods in Hinduism, as I understand it, represent different qualities and aspects.

The importance of understanding this is to know that there is no direct correlation between a physical thing and the underlying quality of which it is an expression. An individual instance of money can be an expression of any number of qualities. Money can be a gift of compassion, a tool of destruction, a means for prolonging life, an instrument of love, and countless other expressions.

So yes, there are qualities, some Divine presence, *underneath* the money. But when you experience money in the world, it's physical. If you're experiencing it as something else, it's no longer money.

I can't use love to buy groceries. But I can express love in how I use money to buy the groceries, choosing where I buy from and how I interact with the people I'm purchasing from. Yet the money itself is physical.

The details are important.

Your Money Story Matters

For simplicity's sake, we humans often try to generalize. "Money is terrible." "I'm bad with debt." The truth is usually far more nuanced and detailed.

Some spiritual teachers would say that "the story" is not important, and that dwelling upon the details of what happened in a particular situation only keeps you stuck.

I see it differently. The Divine has woven a tremendous creation, and each part is unique. Healing is found in the particulars. Our stories contain the deep need to be witnessed: to be truly seen without being judged. And within our stories we can find the pain that reveals where healing is most needed.

When something is uncomfortable enough, we lean away from it. This is natural. Say someone has a debt that they haven't been able to pay off. This common situation elicits all kinds of reactions, most of them uncomfortable or painful. If you're like many of our clients over the years, you'll turn away, saying something like, "I'm terrible with debt."

Instead of turning away, I want to encourage you to face and embrace your situation. As you lean in, you begin to see what's truly going on and things can begin to shift.

First, you realize—not intellectually, as you probably already did, but deep in your heart and being—that the discomfort is not deadly. The emotions are just painful emotions, and you find you can tolerate them.

Second, you now have the opportunity to really look at the debts in your life. Let's imagine you see three specific ones:

1. A student debt, which, no matter how much you pay, doesn't go down.

2. A mortgage you've paid down dependably, which has provided you with a home. Looking back over the mortgage statements, you can see the amount owed dropping steadily.

3. A personal loan from a friend who gave you enough to get lunch one day when you forgot your wallet. You've since paid that friend back.

When you lean in, you realize you're *not* bad with debt. Two out of these three debts are being handled in a healthy way. You've even dealt healthfully with the student loan debt. But in this case, the debt *itself* is unhealthy. There is a predatory interest rate on it, which feels impossible to get around.

These realizations free you to let go of the false generalization, "I'm bad with debt." Instead, you can replace it with the truth, "I tend to handle debt pretty well. *And* there is this one debt that anyone who isn't wealthy would have trouble handling. I need help."

It's a very different story and experience, isn't it? The courage to face the details clears the path to healing.

The healing isn't complete, but you've taken a significant step forward. Can you feel the relief?

Even if the person in question has several debts that have been troublesome, and even if they've dropped the ball and made mistakes with debt, there is a far more honest and nuanced perspective. "I've made mistakes with some debts and not with others. I was never really taught how to handle debt. It's been scary, and I haven't had support. It's not beyond me to deal with debt in a healthy way, but I do need help."

The next steps would be to drop into your heart, in Remembrance or another similar practice, and start to ask, "What does my heart need to be in a healthier relation to this situation?"

Shame Is Not an Emotion

Shame is often closely linked to the topic of money (among many other topics). In the early days of my work with clients, I tried to help them move through the "emotion" of shame. But it was tricky and frequently unsuccessful.

One day I had an insight that has proven quite valuable: shame is not an emotion. There are emotions associated with shame, such as fear, anger, and sadness. But shame itself is not an emotion.

Instead, I understood that shame is a story we tell ourselves to protect our heart. Strange, isn't it?

Often the situation that activates shame is difficult, vulnerable, uncomfortable, and somehow unpredictable. For example, a client told me she felt shame about her work in the world, and this sense of shame kept her from offering her work to new people.

How does shame protect her? Her story of shame is that her work is no good, that she's no good in her essence. What that story does is bring a tremendous amount of certainty to the small "s" self. In believing the story, she's sure that she's no good and neither is her work. With that certainty, she can abandon efforts to promote.

The story is protecting her from the very vulnerable uncertainty of what will happen if she puts her work out to new people. She might get rejected. Some people might not like it. Some people might like it, and then she has responsibility to deliver the work. There's a lot of vulnerability, fear, and uncertainty in that situation.

When we understand shame is a story, when shame comes up for us, we can look for the story. Then we can ask: From what uncertainty or raw uncomfortable emotions (or both) is that story trying to protect us?

When our client faced the story and found the courage to face the uncertainty, she discovered a simple path forward. That path consisted of two things.

First, she was willing to be with uncomfortable emotions. She allowed space in her life to feel them, to express them, to get support and care around them without trying to shut them down or make them all better. In so doing, she discovered that the feelings weren't fatal—that she could face the discomfort in her body and emotions and be okay.

Second, she found and embraced a sincere sense of curiosity. "I wonder what will happen if I put my work out there?" Many people attempt to replace the negative certainty ("I'm going to fail and be rejected!") with a positive certainty ("I'm going to totally fly! It's going to be amazing!"). The truth was, really, that she didn't know. We don't know how something new will turn out. When she embraced the truth of the uncertainty and used curiosity as a way of approaching it, then it all seemed easier and more interesting.

The question, "I wonder …" is such a balm to the heart. It's often the beginning of the path to adventures, discoveries, and successes. And, yes, to failures and mistakes, too. Because it's all part of the path forward.

Curiosity is a critical human capacity. And cultivating curiosity is one of the most powerful antidotes to shame. It shifts the internal narrative in a way that softens judgment and opens the heart to both truth and possibility. Curiosity brings healing.

Being with Discomfort

In this discussion on shame, I touched again on the capacity to face emotional discomfort without the need to fix or soothe. Spiritually speaking, this is one of the most important capacities a human being can develop.

Of course, sometimes we have extreme reactions, due to trauma or other experiences, and our nervous systems do need soothing. We can't live in a state of upset and anxiety.

However, our current culture tends to go to soothing or fixing way too quickly. The simple act of just being present with discomfort—as in, "Oh, this feels terrible. My gut is tight, my shoulders are tense, I'm scared,"—*without* immediately turning to something that soothes the physical body (like the digital world, food, or something else) is often the first and most important step in healing.

Transformation is rooted in the willingness to be in the discomfort that is present without trying to fix it, without telling a story about it, and without trying to cover it over.

Are you angry? Are you terrified? Are you devastated? Are you embarrassed? Can you allow yourself to be with the experience of whatever uncomfortable feeling is coming up?

I believe the capacity to simply be with the truth of our immediate experience (however uncomfortable or painful) is the gateway to wisdom and wholeness, to resilience and love. Being present with discomfort that isn't life-threatening or trauma-inducing opens the door to guidance and true solutions, as opposed to temporary and partial fixes.

Of course, when we do this, we need to be careful about swinging to the other end of the pendulum. We want to avoid sinking into despair in the discomfort, thinking that the pain will never end and it will always be this way.

There is an art and practice to being with the discomfort, to noticing that it doesn't kill us. With deep, gentle breaths and through Remembrance, we ask, "Is love available even here? Is the Divine present even here?"

In this practice, we often find that the distress isn't nearly as intense as we originally thought. Trying to avoid discomfort often amplifies in it in a very painful way. But all on its own, the disquiet we feel usually isn't nearly as bad.

Being willing to simply sit with the discomfort, we can begin to see the situation more clearly. Now the focus is more on wondering what's here and what is being asked, rather than the highest priority being, "Stop the pain!" With this shift, we find ourselves curious about what's needed in the situation and what the way forward might look like: in your financial life, in business, or in any other context.

You Can't Heal from a Distance

Being with discomfort is at the heart of healing. When you stop running from pain, you can see what's really there and begin to see the tasks needed to be freed from it. But if you are struggling with, say, a debt, and find you can't sit with the pain and discomfort that arise when you look at the latest "payment due notice" and the amount written on it, then it's going to be really hard to find your way through.

It can be invaluable to simply sit with the notice open in front of you. Your focus shifts from avoiding pain to establishing a relationship with it. The path of healing and resolution lies directly *through* the topic in question. Distance only prolongs difficulty.

Many are tempted to rush through and simply "get it done," meaning pay the bill, or file the notice, or whatever will create some distance from it in the moment. Yet this is another kind of avoidance. Rapidly paying the minimum on the debt just to get it off your desk and out of sight doesn't solve anything. That's not a plan to clear the debt. That's not reaching out for help from a debt counselor to renegotiate and diminish the debt. That's not sitting with your entire budget and wondering how to rebalance spending priorities. That's not creating a longer-term strategy to grow the revenue of your business so you can pay the debt off more comfortably.

If it's causing that much distress, it's worthy of attention and time.

Financial Tasks as Spiritual Practice

Financial tasks are stressful. Besides the overly complex and legalistic paperwork often involved, financial to-dos can elicit emotional discomfort because they affect our ability to live well and even survive. For these reasons and more, many want to simply "push through."

But financial healing comes when we *make space* for the discomfort.

If you sit down to do spiritual practice or another type of intentional self-improvement exercise, you expect emotions to arise. You expect to feel different feelings, and there's space for that.

However, despite all we know about the emotions that come up during financial tasks, it's rare to give them that kind of space. Instead, many of us say to ourselves, "Ugh, I have to deal with the bills. Let me push through as quickly as I can, so I can just get on to the next, more enjoyable thing."

Imagine for a moment if this were how you dealt with someone you cared about. "Ugh, I have to spend time with my spouse. Let me push through as quickly as I can, so I can get on to the next thing."

In a healthy relationship, we enjoy the good times, and we also show up as fully as possible when things are hard. The required effort to heal any relationship usually lies in *understanding* more before we attempt to take action. If you want a healthy relationship with your finances, it's the same.

What if you were to approach a financial task as a spiritual practice? Allow me to get more specific: What if you were to fully expect emotions, hard emotions, to arise? What if you went into it knowing you were going to feel awkward and distressed at times? What if you included the spaciousness to be with and travel through the emotions, instead of only focusing on "getting it done"?

Imagine what this might look like.

Instead of scheduling just ten minutes to get three or four bills paid online, consider planning for a full hour so as to be present with hard emotions. The extra time would allow *space* for Remembrance; *space* for looking deeply at what is under your reactions; *space* for love, care, healing, and insight.

What might that hour look like? Imagine picking up one of the bills and really being with how uncomfortable it makes you feel. Maybe it's a debt you owe for something you don't think you should owe or for something you regret purchasing. There's grief and anger and sadness there, and all these emotions need space. Settled into that space, and simply willing to be with all the feelings that arise, you can ask: "What does my heart need to be in a healthier relationship with this debt?"

Now, this is, of course, unsustainable in the long run. For most of us, it's difficult if not impossible to slot in an hour to pay some bills. Our lives are very full, and we will get run down if we spend all that extra time every week doing tasks that could happen more quickly.

Remember, though, that pushing through or avoiding isn't going to be effective for truly changing the way money is working in your life. And there is good news. If you take the time at first, it gets easier and faster later on, as the emotional tangles are cleared out of your heart.

In fact, if you approach these tasks as I described above once, twice, three times, you'll start to clear the backlog of spiritual and emotional confusion and pain. It will all start to move more easily. You will get to the point where you can indeed just spend ten minutes paying the bills, but without the stress and anxiety that had been weighing you down before.

Next, I want to address a topic common in business, especially with money: neediness.

Neediness Is Healthy

So often neediness is discussed as a negative. "Don't be needy." We judge ourselves and others for displays of neediness. Much of Western culture tells us to be independent of needs, to be "do it yourselfers."

Here's a little-acknowledged historical fact: The term "Pull yourself up by your own bootstraps" was originally coined in the late 1800s to refer to an impossible task. In our dysfunctional culture, it has been twisted into something celebrated, even expected. But no one can pull themselves up by their own bootstraps. No one is truly independent of need.

We are all needy. We cannot manufacture the air we need to breathe, the water we need to drink. We cannot manufacture the food we eat, although we can be part of the support it needs to grow.

When we feel hunger, the healthy reaction is not to judge ourselves. Rather, we simply feed ourselves.

The essence of the human being, according to Sufism, is neediness. The feeling of neediness that arises in us, as uncomfortable as it is, is simply our awareness of ourselves as a vessel to be filled.

I have a glass of water on the desk in front of me as I write. The essence of the glass is the emptiness of the vessel. It becomes useful to me in my thirst when it is full and I can drink from it. But its fullness in any moment, or its emptiness in another, doesn't change the basic *is*-ness of the glass, which is an empty vessel.

If we're going to receive any kind of goodness, then the emptiness, the neediness, is absolutely necessary. For if you're full, how can you receive more? There have been many versions of the story told where a spiritual seeker comes to the master asking to become a student and learn. The master pours a cup of tea but doesn't stop when the cup is full, and it overflows onto the table and the floor. "What are you doing?" the student asks, upset. "If the cup is already full, how can anything else be added?" comes the reply. The master speaks of the empty state, the state of neediness, which creates the capacity to receive.

There is an oral Sufi teaching I've received from my teachers. The teaching says, "The aim is not to drink to quench your thirst. The aim is to develop the perfect thirst, so that you never stop drinking."

The emotional discomfort I referenced above—that is, the distress that arises in facing financial tasks—is an echo of this. It's a sign of thirst, of neediness. The distress is akin to the telltale sensation of thirst in your throat, or perhaps the rumble of hunger in your belly. This emotional discomfort is a healthy sign! It tells you that you have a good and legitimate need and that you are empty enough to receive.

The challenge, of course, is what I've also described above. It isn't easy to be with the neediness, the discomfort, without seeking immediately to fix it, soothe it, fill it.

Every year, I practice the monthlong daylight fast of Ramadan, which has helped me develop this capacity. I'm fortunate enough that my health allows me to do this without harm. I can feel hunger and thirst and not panic. I have learned deeply that I can go hours with hunger and thirst and not collapse.

This knowledge has many benefits. The one I want to underscore here is the benefit of knowing I *can* slow down; I *can* carry this discomfort with patience; and I *do* have the time to seek out truly nourishing food. When I'm fasting, it's more important than ever that the two meals I take in (one before dawn, and one at twilight) be as healthy and nourishing as possible.

You can develop this capacity around your emotional neediness. You can learn to meet your discomfort with patience. You can take the time to discern what your heart truly needs: what would be truly nourishing. This can be so liberating because it means you are developing the patience, persistence, and awareness to work toward what you, your business, and your finances truly need to be healthy.

Also, you will be doing yourself a tremendous spiritual service by stepping into a healthier relationship with neediness. You will know that you are neither bad nor broken for having neediness. Embracing your neediness is, in fact, one of the surest pathways to spiritual truth, nourishment, and abundance.

EXERCISE

Your Heart and Money

Here is an exercise from our program, Heart of Money and Power Transformational Journey. If you would like me to lead you through it, you can access the guided recording here.

www.heartcenteredbusinessbook.com/resources/your-heart-and-money

1. **Start with the Remembrance in your heart.**

2. **Ask the Divine to bring the essence of money in front of your heart.** You can use whatever image or feeling you need to; for example, some people use images of cash, coins, or checkbooks. Notice how you react to it. Let yourself really feel your reaction. How does your heart react to the presence of money?

   Tip: Don't get too hung up about what image you use. Just make sure it's an image of money you see in your everyday life.

   Example: I brought a stack of twenties in front of my heart and immediately felt my heart cringe and back away—how surprising! I thought I wanted more money! My heart felt scared and gun-shy—very painful.

3. **Ask yourself: What is under this reaction?** I have found that most but not all people have more than one layer of reaction. Let yourself feel what is in this next layer.

Tip: Don't get hung up with words like layer or deep. It's just about allowing yourself to identify the emotions that come up. Let yourself breathe through the layers of emotion. And as you become familiar with each emotion, let your heart show you as many layers as you have.

Example: As I sat in Remembrance and felt shyness and fear, I began to feel a rage bubbling underneath all of it. I let myself feel the rage, continued the Remembrance, and realized there was a deep sadness under the rage. The sadness, almost a despair, felt like the bottom to me—it was really black and empty down there. I could only stay with it using the Remembrance.

4. **Then, ask to be shown what Divine quality or qualities are being nurtured, developed, or unveiled for you through your experience with money.**

Tip: Divine qualities come in an infinite number of flavors. Don't worry about whether yours is the "right" one. Just be curious about what is being strengthened in you.

Your reactions are only the twisting of the Divine qualities. Beneath those reactions, what is the clear essence of the quality that is being brought out in you?

Example: This took a while. As I sat in Remembrance with the despair, I began to feel a warmth in my belly and my heart, and I began to feel much stronger and more confident. In asking the question, I began feeling a core-level strength growing inside of me. This is huge!

5. **Drink in this quality.** Ask for help in receiving it. Let it come through and into your body. Silently repeat the name or sense of this quality in your heart.

Tip: I'm using the "drink" metaphor. You may experience this quality as light, as a feeling, or just as a noticing. Focus on how the presence of the quality feels in your body and/ or your heart. What if that feeling permeated your body? Really allow it to come in. How does it feel as you fill with this quality?

Example: In Remembrance, I continued letting this strength come in. I've never felt so solid before in my lower body. It was the first time I've been able to feel genuine gratitude for all my money challenges. I can now see that I'm really turning a corner.

6. **From this place of receiving, ask yourself: What is one new thing the Divine would like you to take on in creating a healthier relationship with money? Let yourself be in a place of not knowing, of curiosity, of willingness to be surprised as you ask in your heart.**

Tip: Make this step a doable action. "Be more grateful" can't be put in a calendar. "Spend five minutes at the end of each day listing all I'm grateful for," can be put in a calendar.

Example: I could see that it's finally time to get on top of my quarterly business taxes. With this strength, I felt willing to ask for help—I plan to call a friend for a referral to an accountant, and maybe in the next few weeks, with their help, I could come up with a plan for saving and sending in my quarterly estimated taxes.

As you take on more of this Divine Essence quality in your life, as each step is given to you, your relationship to money will express other facets of your relationship with the Beloved.

As you undertake this exercise, you may notice two things in addition to any insights that arise. First, any number of things can replace "money" in the exercise. In fact, you can use this exercise to help pinpoint what your heart needs to have a healthier relationship with any aspect of your business or your life.

Second, the emotional discomfort associated with this practice can be significant. It can be incredibly helpful to find a friend—someone you deeply trust—to hold a space of Remembrance or openheartedness with and for you, without trying to manage or fix you. This person could help you by prompting you through the exercise's steps and by holding a patient, open spaciousness as you take whatever time you need.

It's a commonly observed experience that spiritual practice done with others brings greater ease and depth. The same is true with these kinds of exercises. You can absolutely do wonderful work on your own. *And*, if you're able, having a friend to accompany you can be very beneficial.

✿

Things to Remember:

- Money is physical. As such, it can represent or carry a variety of different significant spiritual or emotional meanings depending on the context.
- Healing is in the details, and your story matters. By giving attention to the details, you can heal an individual situation and find a deeper truth that applies more broadly.
- Shame is not an emotion. It's an untrue, unnuanced story that is protecting you from more uncomfortable raw emotions.
- Take on uncomfortable financial tasks as a spiritual practice, giving time and space to be with uncomfortable emotions rather than trying to rush through them.
- Neediness is healthy. It's a sign of openness and emptiness that allows you to receive, and it is a doorway to profound healing.

CHAPTER 3

You Can Be Trusted with Your Business

M any people just don't trust themselves. Again and again at Heart of Business, we see this painful sense of inner distrust affecting our clients' businesses and lives.

For instance, a client was faced with someone asking her to collaborate on a project. Our client didn't have a good feeling about this alliance. However, she found herself thinking maybe she *should* work with this person because it was a "good idea."

On the face of it, it did appear to be a good idea. This other person had a sizeable audience, which would benefit our client. The potential collaborator also wasn't a competitor to our client because they offered something very different.

However, our client said it just didn't feel right. She trusted her own intuition enough to notice her unease and bring it up. But saying no to the opportunity required more support. And she got that support from our community.

Was our client overlooking a big opportunity? Should she have said yes? Or would saying yes have run roughshod over her deeper and wiser intuition to steer clear?

The answer? It's complicated.

I began the last two chapters by affirming that there is wisdom in any reaction you might have to the topics of business or money, however intense or negative. Supporting clients in listening to their own heart is a significant part of my work. I want them to trust themselves deeply.

I want that profound self-trust for you, too. Let's talk about this.

Trusting the small-s "self" is not always a straightforward proposition. We don't want to be prisoners of our fears and prejudices. There's a lot of research that describes how bias shows up unconsciously. It's not healthy or helpful to just run with every stray thought that arises for us. At the same time, we don't want to harm ourselves by suppressing or otherwise ignoring those impulses.

Our client who had a bad feeling about a possible business collaboration? *All* her doubts were worthwhile—even her doubts about her doubts! See, trusting ourselves means trusting that anything that arises is worth paying attention to more closely. This does not mean taking everything that comes up for us at face value and just following it. Our client both had a "not good feeling" and also doubted that "not good feeling." An inner conflict like this is particularly hard to navigate because it threatens a no-win situation: whether she ignores her not-good feeling or ignores her doubts about it, she is not honoring her own heart's truth.

In this life, it's incredibly helpful to learn to trust yourself in every moment so that you can find the wisdom and insight that is present, often below the surface of any initial reaction. And I do mean in *every* moment. Unapologetic, unrelenting self-trust is the seemingly impossible task I want to undertake in this chapter.

A Misunderstood Spiritual Teaching about Trust

There is a spiritual teaching that says, "Everything is from the Divine." This teaching is often misunderstood—and, at times, misused—in quite harmful ways.

According to the Sufis and many other spiritual paths, the origin of everything that exists is the Source, the Oneness, what some call the Divine or God.

This reality of everything arising from the Divine is both the reason why we can trust ourselves deeply and the reason we need a lot of nuance in how we apply that trust.

Because we've been trained by modern culture to categorize things as "other," it's challenging to really "get" that the Divine is *not* an external being, *not* a so-called "beard in the sky." The Source of all cannot be a thing among things; otherwise, it would not be the Source of all things. We ourselves are expressions of the Divine Source, and yet we do not comprise the entirety of Source.

I want to explain the two broad ways that people have Divine experiences, so that we can understand their roles in a nuanced trusting of ourselves. The two ways that we tend to experience Divine presence are *immanence* and *transcendence*.

Immanent means experiencing the Divine within. It's feeling that profound sense of love in your own heart. It's inwardly knowing you aren't separate in any way and there are vast worlds within.

Transcendent means experiencing the Divine coming to you from outside, or "descending" into (or onto) you. Here you feel held, or carried, or loved, or taught, or guided, or empowered, or inspired by an external Divine Source.

Theologians sometimes argue about whether the Divine is transcendent or immanent. But people who have experienced these states know they both contain truth.

According to the Sufis, nothing exists without the Divine presence. The Source is a reality that interpenetrates everything: that *is* all of time and space and also *outside* time and space.

We can taste or perceive that reality in our own hearts, and it is wondrous. People who have had extended experiences of Divine immanence and transcendence say it's life-changing. They know that love is available everywhere and there is a deep trust and peace that lives within them.

There are times when we look within ourselves to find that presence, to find it arising out of our own heart. Then we come to know, without a doubt, that we do carry the love within.

There are also times when we're feeling small and separate. Disconnected. The reconnection to love can then sometimes feel as if the Divine is descending on us, coming to us from outside, as the illusion of separation melts and we reconnect.

The thoughts and reactions we have arise from these same places within, from a Divine Source. That carries an inherent trustworthiness with it.

However, because our perceptions can become tangled or difficult to interpret due to our experience of disconnection, the initial understanding of any thought or reaction that arises can't necessarily be taken at face value.

I love both the immanent and the transcendent. I'm all in favor of you having as many ways to the Divine as possible, of knowing that every path leads to the Source of love.

When one says, "Everything is from the Divine," it means that the origin of everything's existence is this Source and that the Divine can be accessed everywhere. Sometimes we perceive it as arising internally; sometimes we perceive it as arriving from elsewhere. The reality is that it's already there, and it's our perception that is changing: opening, widening, deepening to perceive it.

This is what I mean when I say you can trust everything that arises within you, that everything is worth listening to more deeply.

Our client who had conflicting feelings about collaboration is a great example of this. She wanted to collaborate, and her instincts to collaborate were arising from wisdom, but her desire to collaborate with this person had cautions with it, and she needed to listen to those.

I want to speak to a little-understood spiritual state that is important to this topic of self-trust. Of listening with deeper inquiry.

Love in the Disconnect

I remember being with my Sufi teachers at an immersive week-long retreat. I had been named as a first-level Sufi teacher already, but I was still feeling young and inexperienced in many ways.

One night there was a *dhikr*, which is a word that literally means "Remembrance." It's a gathering of chanting, held in a circle, where we as a group become one voice, one breath in remembrance of the Divine. It's a beautiful practice. That night there were well over one hundred of us present, and it was powerful.

In these cases, there's a teacher who stands in the middle of the circle, like the conductor. When the group is very large, there are often helper teachers who keep the group connected and individuals grounded during chanting.

As we began the first chant, I noticed that the main teacher was pulling other teachers in to help. As you can imagine, I very much wanted to be pulled in, too. This feeling spiraled out of control with me, and I kept *not* being picked. Even the person standing next to me was pulled in. Not me.

A very strong feeling of disconnection arose in me. I felt unseen, unappreciated, and so distant—like an outsider. I kept chanting, but my thoughts were spiraling in this way. I was trying to remember the Divine, and trying to connect, *and* trying to be noticed. I was a mess inside.

Then, through nothing I did, there was a moment of opening inside me. I still felt distant; I still felt unseen by others, separate, outside. Yet there was a powerful feeling that this distance I was feeling was *also*, somehow, the Divine. I felt the love *in* the distance, *in* the disconnection.

It's hard to put into words, but it turned my heart upside down in a good way and brought me to a very deep surrender in that moment. It gave me a taste that the love is present everywhere, and the love doesn't always feel like yummy intimacy.

I lost a sense of myself and instead felt myself just moving with the Oneness, with the Remembrance. It felt like I was being moved and being chanted.

It was, of course, at that moment that I, as a teacher, was pulled into the circle to help support our Remembrance. I was pulled in when I didn't care about being pulled in—when it no longer meant anything to me, other than that was where I was being placed. The thing I had so wanted had become immaterial to me. It didn't matter where I stood; my heart was content in the love.

The feeling of connection eventually subsided when the dhikr wound down some time later, but it lived on in my heart, and I've had other experiences like that since.

The disconnected state does not mean love is not present. It only means we may need to expand our understanding of love. We may be perceiving love to only look or feel a certain way. But because Divine love is truly infinite, there is no place, no time, no situation, where love is absent.

This story of love in the disconnection is an example of why we need to trust ourselves deeply. The disconnection that arose within me was not useful at face value. For me to have just thought of myself as disconnected and uncared for—and trusted that thought—would have been so damaging to my heart. And ultimately false.

However, because I was in that dhikr circle, it wasn't possible for me to shut down or otherwise ignore the feeling, and I was aware enough of my own reactions that I couldn't embrace it at face value, either.

Instead, I was carried inwardly, immanently, more deeply. There was wisdom in the feeling of disconnection; there was truth there. But ironically, I couldn't trust my own surface interpretation of that feeling. Instead, I needed to trust that feeling of distance and disconnection because it was leading me to the profound discovery of love in the disconnection itself.

Similarly, with our client, she needed to slow down so she could listen to both of her reactions—the wanting to collaborate, and the inner warning that the collaboration didn't feel good—to find a deeper truth.

What eventually emerged out of honoring all of it? She saw that she hadn't always been good about making her own needs known in these kinds of relationships. She realized she had let others set the terms, and she'd often ended up not receiving benefit or support from the collaboration.

As she saw that and told me, I supported her in identifying what her needs and desires were around the collaboration. As she owned those needs and desires, she felt a strength in her heart, and the not-good feeling about the collaboration melted. In this instance, it hadn't been an intuition that the other person would be a harmful person with whom to collaborate. Rather, the mixture of feelings helped her identify the deeper truth, which was that the collaboration could be good if she were willing to allow her own strengths and desires to be present.

More importantly (and beyond this individual collaboration), my client learned that she could trust all that arose within her and allow it to help her find the healthy path forward.

Finding this deeper truth, which often lies in between two extremes (Collaborate! No, don't collaborate!) is what we sometimes call "the middle path."

The Middle Path of Marketing

Here's a second example to help what I'm saying take root within you. As is very common, one of our clients had a revulsion toward marketing. The middle path says they shouldn't just take that revulsion at face value and avoid all marketing. Nor should they take the other extreme and tell themselves, "My revulsion toward marketing is just some belief I need to get over or change."

What might this middle path look like?

I asked the client, "What if you could really trust yourself? What if you could view the revulsion as a reflection of something true, but at the same time, not take it fully at face value? What if you could listen more deeply—with curiosity, trust, and openness?"

She was brave enough to lean in, to embrace the revulsion, and to honor her own reaction. She reported her whole body relaxing when she realized that she could trust her response, and simply listen to what it might be teaching her. And as she attended to her heart's entire message, she realized it wasn't merely "revulsion at all marketing." Rather, she'd had a justifiable revulsion to *unethical* marketing, which was something she had experienced as a consumer. Her heart was refusing to perpetrate the deep wrong of which she had been an unfortunate recipient.

But she also felt a yearning to be seen in her business, a desire to be of service to people who really needed her skills and experience. She was able to embrace the wisdom of the revulsion, the truth in the yearning, and to open her heart to learning new ways of being with marketing. She was able to make her business visible while trusting that she wouldn't allow herself to fall into unethical marketing practices.

Of course, that wasn't the end of it all. Revulsion and resistance would continue to pop up. But she learned she could listen instead of flatly rejecting it, fighting it, or following it. She learned to thread a pathway through the business world that was made up partly with teachings she trusted, partly with her own intuition, and partly with her strong sense of justice and ethics.

In trusting this process of integration, she also became adept at resisting the allure of "get-rich-quick" methods that promised to fix all her marketing problems. With her heart she could see through those false promises and simply let them go.

The Truth Within

The process of learning to trust your reactions, and to seek love even through feelings of disconnection, is beautiful. I will warn you, however: more than one person has gone through this process with us and learned to love marketing and even business as they came to understand it with their own hearts.

This is what I mean when I say, "you can trust yourself," and "everything comes from the Divine." Anything that arises in you can only arise because it contains at least a seed of truth.

According to the Sufis, the Divine is also called *al Haqq*, the Truth. This true reality, the Real, is at the heart of everything that exists.

Business versus Spiritual

Sometimes we're struggling with conflicting internal feelings that help us to find a deeper message, like the examples above.

In other cases, however, it's not about the interplay of different beliefs; it's about the age-old conflict of inner versus outer. In this context of business, it looks like this: Do you work on your (inner) heart alignment, or do you work on making your (outer) marketing message clearer? Do you have trouble (inwardly) receiving, or are you unclear about how to (outwardly) hold an effective sales conversation with integrity?

It is common in spiritual circles to privilege the "spiritual" over the physical form. However, from a Sufi point of view, this is a big mistake on a few different levels. As we shall see, it can also have negative implications for business practices.

The first and most fundamental mistake is thinking that our internal experiences are somehow more spiritual than the physical world. This belief has allowed many supposedly devout religious people to create industries and businesses that destroy the earth and/or hurt other people. "Kill 'em all and let God sort them out," is an extreme version of this. There is danger and violence in this belief that the material world is spiritually inferior.

The Divine is in everything. And this really means *everything*. It includes your inner heart, and it includes sales conversations. It includes the deep experience you had on a retreat, and it includes your invoicing and accounting system. There is nothing that is not from the love.

The second mistake in this belief is the assumption that a connection with the Divine requires solely a consistent internal effort of willpower. The truth is that our connection also includes profound support in the physical world.

The Sufis use the analogy of a tree, which has both the sap that flows within and the bark on the outside. Without the bark, the tree is not protected, and the sap cannot flow. Girdling a tree, meaning to damage the bark in a full circumference, will kill the tree, because it blocks the flow of sap.

For an Islamic Sufi, one of the practices is to pray five times a day. Simply trying to remember internally to make that connection is not realistic. By the way, the Arabic word that is often translated as "prayer" in English, *salat*, means "connection." The language is "make salat" or "make connection.

In Muslim culture, you hear the call to prayer, called the *adan*, when it's time to stop and pray, called in a beautiful way from a nearby mosque. For me, not living in that culture, I have an app on my phone that interrupts my day with the adan.

That outer structure—the phone, the app—brings the call to my ears. It cuts through whatever I'm doing, asking me to stop, remember, and connect to the love.

The rules of religion can be terrible if they are used in a harmful way. However, there are many guidelines in the practice of spirituality that are intended as helpful structures, supporting us to turn our attention and experience back to the Source of love and deepening our ability to carry it. I would struggle so much to develop my own heart's capacity for love if I had to do it on will power alone. Structure has helped deepen my inner reality.

This privileging of the inner spiritual over the outer structure, which is also spiritual, undermines so much trust in oneself. We've had so many clients come to us over the years, saying, "I have an issue with spiritually receiving, and I'm sure this is why I have no clients—I'm just not open enough in my heart to receiving more. I keep working on it but I just can't heal it."

These beautiful beloveds are struggling to make themselves better, somehow. They believe the receiving part of their heart is broken. I ask them, "Before we look at that, I want to explore what your business looks like." Usually what is revealed is that their message isn't clear, their offer isn't clear, and they don't know how to hold a focused sales conversation with integrity and effectiveness.

When we put these outer structures in place, they find that they can get clients. And yes, they might still have discomfort with receiving that needs healing at a spiritual level. But it's not nearly as huge as they had believed it to be.

The opposite is also true. A client of ours was marketing a seminar and had done all the right things. Good messaging, good offer, right pricing, confidence and clarity in holding a sales conversation—all the things. But his class wasn't filling up.

When we looked, we found that his heart was closed, he was feeling desperate, and he was trying too hard to make it happen. When he found a place of surrender in his heart, moved toward genuine service and care, and extended a message of love, the floodgates opened overnight. He had to book a larger room.

Now, this is not a typical result. I rarely see this kind of overnight "flip the switch" response from spiritual work, although it does happen. More typically, when people realign their heart and immerse themselves in love, the *quality* of their communication changes significantly, even if their actions are similar. What they write has no "push" in it. Their conversations with potential clients are full of humility, service, and care, without any energy of "taking." Thus, people respond quite differently. The strategies they put into their businesses then start to work.

What I want to emphasize is that spirituality, connection, and love are in everything, whether internal or external. Structure supports and expresses spirit, while spirit supports and informs structure. Sometimes we need to lean into one first, sometimes the other.

On Terrible, Unethical Business

The presence of evil in our world—in business and beyond—is a profound and disturbing mystery. A business book is not the place to delve deeply into those waters.

What can be said is that we humans are far from perfect. Our perceptions are imperfect and our understandings incomplete. Naturally, our actions arising out of these perceptions and understandings are flawed and sometimes cause harm.

For the Sufis, one place harmful human actions arise from is a lack of clarity. The goal of the human journey is to polish the mirror of our hearts, so that we can perceive the reality, the love, more and more clearly. The idea of polishing the mirror comes from a time when mirrors weren't silvered glass but polished metal. Over time, these metal mirrors became tarnished, sometimes rusting, which distorted and obscured the reflection. Regular polishing kept the surface smooth and the reflection as accurate as possible.

The Sufis believe that the heart is the mirror of the Real. We polish it by undertaking practices that help us remember love, increase humility, deepen vulnerability, and nurture sincerity. In this manner, the more beautiful qualities of the Divine can be carried and reflected within us.

Unethical marketers act without a commitment to integrity and care. Their mirror is tarnished, and they lack the desire and/or skill to polish it and so gain a connection to the truth of love. The damage caused by their unethical business actions is significant.

Over the years, my partner Holly and I have lived in several different homes. Sometimes my office has been in the basement, with windows at ground level. Inevitably these windows became dirty, covered with mud, and overgrown with weeds. I had to work consistently and diligently to keep the windows clear. Sometimes even on sunny, bright, blue-sky days, the world outside my basement windows looked muddy and obscured, with only a fraction of light making its way into the office.

The mud-splattered windows affected my mood, my outlook, my expression. The mud on the panes obscured the sense of hope and promise that the bright sun and the brilliant, beautiful day might have bestowed upon me.

Is it the case that love, truth, and divinity are (somehow) still at the core of what these unethical marketers are doing? Yes. But the love has been so obscured, distorted, and veiled by the mud of disconnection that their actions often end up expressing truth's exact opposite.

Strategy and Heart

The topic of distorted marketing brings me to the question of business strategy. So many of our heart-centered business owners recoil at the idea of being strategic, especially around relationships. "I don't want to just use people for their connections!"

Right! Yes! Please don't!

Being strategic does not necessarily mean you're using people. Rather, strategy is simply another word for being intentional and focused. The sales conversation, for instance, is one place I often observe a lack of strategy with those I mentor. One individual had a history of holding two-hour sales conversations with potential clients. She would end up feeling like she'd made a friend and had a great social time. Yet no paying client emerged.

She wasn't being intentional, strategic, in these conversations. What was really going on? This client of mine had been working very hard on her business and was feeling disconnected from friends. Unconsciously, she was using these sales conversations to meet her social needs. This was working to some degree. But she wasn't emerging with true friends that were going to be part of her inner social circle.

And, equally problematic, she wasn't providing focused attention to potential clients and the issues they were facing. With a bit of strategy—focused intentionality—the conversations could have been used to help people by connecting their unique need with her unique service. Instead of using up two hours of a stranger's time (not to mention her own), she could have spent only thirty to forty-five minutes and emerged with a grateful, paying client who could get help with their problem.

Strategy helps by focusing intention to *everyone's* benefit.

In addition, business owners often find their inner intuitions alone to be vague, confusing, and unstructured. Strategic business tactics and "how-tos" provide a backdrop to use *with* intuition. For instance, imagine you're a highly trained and skilled surgeon. If you *also* have a highly developed sense of inward guidance and intuition, you are probably going to be an even better surgeon. Your depth, nuance, and sensitivity help you make the best use of the technical knowledge, abilities, and experience you possess.

However, no matter how highly attuned your sense of intuition is, if you don't also have training in surgery, please keep that scalpel away from me.

I often have clients start with strategy: the practical lessons. Many of them have had more experience accessing their heart than learning about business. So I like to see them fill in the deficit. When they learn a new heart-centered business tactic or skill, then they can use their heart to digest and iterate it. Over time, they can make the strategy an expression of who they are by listening to and trusting themselves.

It's true that when we learn something new, there is almost inevitably a process of "monkey see, monkey do." It's natural to learn unfamiliar skills through imitation. But it needn't take long for intuition and heart to integrate with the new, strategic skill set.

For instance, at Heart of Business, we have a template called the Basic Eight Pages that helps clients approach the content on their websites. These eight pages are one way to meet what we see as the primary questions and needs of new visitors when they first arrive at your website.

Most of our clients follow the template of the Basic Eight the first time through. They bring their creativity to how they express themselves, but they don't change the structure. Many of them are happy there, and they don't change anything further.

Others—after they've digested the intentions and principles behind the Basic Eight and gained clarity about their own audience—begin to use their intuition and creativity to change up the structure as well.

Strategy should never be ascendant over your own intuition. At the same time, you should never discard strategy learned from a trusted source if it's in an area of business that you haven't yet learned about.

No Formulas

When faced with a challenge involving significant risk, we humans often seek certainty as a way of creating safety. This is surely true in business, where what's at stake is often financial survival and the ability to express one's gifts, among other important elements in life.

Seeking certainty often means seeking a formula. If I do X and Y in a particular way, then I'll get Z result.

This doesn't work in business, and this doesn't work in spirituality. In business, it's called "paint by numbers" and never gets consistent results. In spirituality, I call it "vending machine spirituality" where one puts in a prayer and expects to receive, as the equivalent of a candy bar, whatever one was praying for.

The more trustworthy and certain path lies in approaching business, life, and spirituality with the understanding that they're not mechanical but relational. This way forward can seem more tedious, especially to a troubled mind. Yet when we take the time to listen and sift, to relate in our hearts to what we're facing, then what our hearts truly need is revealed. And when we receive what our hearts need, then we can step forward.

You can be trusted. Deeply. All that arises within you can be trusted. You can find the truth, if you can take the risk of slowing down, listening, and sorting out the nuance of what's really being expressed to you.

I promise you this. If you relate to it all—your business, the marketplace, the strategy, and all the people who surround your business—with a heart rooted in the Source of love, you will find a trustworthy path forward that is all your own.

Things to Remember:
- Everything that arises in you is trustworthy, with a Divine origin within. Contradictory feelings mean that nuance needs to be discerned, while all feelings and ideas are honored.
- The things that do arise in you may not be helpful at face value. The deeper listening of the heart can help to reveal what's really needed.
- The inner reality—what many call the "spiritual experience"—is not inherently superior or more spiritual than the physical world. Many times, outer structures and events support a deeper spiritual connection in surprising and powerful ways.
- There are not set formulas, except to take the time to listen and discern. Although it can seem like it moves more slowly, in the end it is far more efficient to discern the full truth before taking significant action.

CHAPTER 4

The First Two Stages of Business Development

Years ago, we had somebody come to us and say, "You know, I'm starting up my business, and I want to get a website. The website designer quoted me ten thousand dollars for a new site. Is this a reasonable amount?"

My response was, "No way. Stop. Don't spend that much. It doesn't make any sense. When you invest too much too early in your business, you can totally overwhelm it. You'd never get a six-month-old baby fitted for a custom tuxedo for thousands of dollars, because in three months it's not going to fit, right? Same principle applies."

In addition to these kinds of questions, in Heart of Business's early days, I was also confronting the ever-present challenge for our clients: there is way too much to do to get a business going. So many, many things.

There are skills to learn, systems and structures to implement, and emotions to work with. Even in a tiny, one-person business, there's *a lot*. And it's compounded by everyone in the world trying to sell you some sexy thing for your business, like a ten-thousand-dollar website.

Since it's impossible to do it all at once, what do you do first? Most people focus on what they are most comfortable with. The problem, of course, is that what you're most comfortable with is rarely what the business needs at the moment. Plus, there are pieces you may never be comfortable with (or maybe don't even know about), so they don't get done. This is a haphazard way of approaching business.

Let me introduce a less haphazard, more effective, and way less overwhelming way forward.

A Developmental Approach

Over the years, I have come to a developmental understanding of microbusinesses. Such businesses have a particular path of development—a path that isn't generally discussed in MBA programs or other professional business settings.

The developmental approach can seem daunting. It can be challenging to see the reality of where your business actually is, often much earlier in development than you hoped, and consequently what needs to be put in place to make it stable enough to support you. Truthfully, it takes longer to get there than you've perhaps been told.

A lot of slick marketers want to sell you on the "get to six figures in six weeks, or six months, or one year!" or whatever their program says. This is not a fair expectation of anyone. In twenty years of business coaching, I can count the number of times I've seen that happen on one hand. It's not anything to depend on.

A very important gift the developmental model brings to you in bucket loads—ocean-loads, even—is compassion.

Most small business owners believe their businesses are broken because they aren't yet financially profitable enough to meet their needs. They end up believing there is something fundamentally wrong with their business, or even with themselves. It's painful for me to witness this belief.

The truth is that for most of them—and most likely, you—their business is *not* broken.

Let me ask you a question. If you were with a six-year-old child, and they were unable to read a novel, or drive a car, or pay the rent, would you think there was something deeply wrong with the child?

Of course not. You would understand that the kid is too young to be that skilled or productive. Wait five or ten or fifteen years, and the child will grow more and more into the fullness of all they will ultimately be capable of.

The child isn't broken. They just need to grow and develop.

When our twin boys were four or five, they tried to help us clean. But actually, it made more work for us—even if it was joyful. We could not expect them to really clean. Now, as young teens, their help in maintaining our household is deeply appreciated and quite significant. They needed to grow into it.

You get the point I'm making. Most small businesses (including yours) are not broken. They are simply at an earlier stage of development and can't be expected to do everything at once.

For many, this brings real relief and compassion. Compassion for yourself, knowing that there's nothing wrong with you for taking the time that it takes. And compassion for your business, knowing that it's not really broken—nothing is really *wrong*—it's just developing.

Your business needs to grow into its potential if it's to develop into something that really can support you. This becomes so much easier when you see the sequence of development. When you put certain things in place first, it brings stability to the business and makes later elements *much* more manageable.

There are two things that make this fun—and easier than you might expect. The first thing is that, unlike a human being, it doesn't take a business eighteen years, or even eight years, to fully develop, if you're focused on development. It generally takes three to five years to move your business fully into Momentum.

The other truth that makes this fun is that you do *not* chug along with zero results, then *boom*, at the end, suddenly it starts working. Instead, every element that gets put in place creates results. So you see results every step along the way, and you get to really experience how each of the elements supports the others.

It's a wonderful, nourishing journey, as well as a frustrating, painful journey at times. But it's made more wonderful (and less painful) when you know where to place your focus now and what you can successfully put off until later.

And building a heart-centered business can be even more nourishing because most business tasks are integrated within spiritual understandings that help to anchor you solidly into your own heart.

How Long Does It Really Take?

It takes time to get to Momentum in business. In the years that Heart of Business has been working with people, I've observed thousands of businesses evolve. On average, moving from the First Stage to the Third Stage of business development takes from eighteen months to four years of steady focus and effort.

When you're creating a business that's really going to sustain you, it's incredibly helpful to know the arc, understand the stages, and accept that you're playing the long game. With these pieces in view, you can really have some fun growing your business. You know where to focus, as well as how to invest your money, time, and energy.

If you want to get your business to a sustainable level, it is necessary to go through these three stages. Stage Four, Independence, is optional, and significantly different than the previous three stages, as I will explain later.

Oh, and one more thing. Most of the elements in each of the four stages are iterative. This means that they are not "one and done." Instead, you work with each element just enough to make it effective for where you are, then you move on. Later, you will inevitably circle back to improve and iterate the elements as your business develops.

This is true of our journey in life and of any spiritual development we pursue along the way. Rarely is anything "one and done." At one point I learned to play the guitar at an extremely basic level. I found that learning chords and learning songs was iterative in this same way. I would learn one way to make a chord. Then as I put chords together into songs, I learned different ways to hold the same chord. For instance, I think I learned at least three different ways to make a D chord. Each version had a different sound or a different use, depending on the song I was playing. With every step forward in my guitar playing—which, honestly, never progressed very far—I kept returning to the basics.

Spiritually we may discover a depth in our heart, then discover that there is even more depth available. We encounter a block, an old trauma, and we bring compassion and healing to it. As it untangles, we have more spaciousness in ourselves. Yet we often hit the same block again, then again, untangling it more at each iteration.

As it all untangles, we find a softness and gentleness in ourselves that blossoms into a richness. Then we return and find strength that deepens and solidifies us. And compassion, with an ability to witness others, that opens and opens.

We keep returning to the heart, and to our businesses, and see each aspect develop more and more. So let that be your guiding inspiration through the stages: effective, not perfect, knowing you will come back and improve different business elements time and again.

The First Stage: Creation

A business in Creation is missing all the basics that make it easy to have clients come in. There's a lack of clarity in describing what the business is, and a lack of focus and confidence in connecting with new potential clients. Often this business is bringing in nothing or almost nothing, financially. The business owner can feel at a loss about how to even get the business going.

It should be said that one can be in business for quite some time, months or years even, and still be in the First Stage. Occasionally a business will do well even in the First Stage.

We've had clients over the years that have exited a corporate job to become a consultant, and their former employer became their first consulting client. They had good money coming in for a while, even a couple of years, then, when the contract finished up, they realized belatedly that they had not put any business development elements in place. They were shocked to find they were starting completely from scratch, even though financially, and workload wise, it had looked like they had a successful consulting business.

There's no shame in being in Creation, even if you've been at it awhile. No one told you! So let me describe this stage so that you know how to move through it.

The real focus of Stage One is play and experimentation. It may seem ridiculous to focus on play and exploration straight away. After all, you probably need to bring in money, and your hopes and dreams are riding on it. I really get it. I've been through this and have walked with countless clients here as well. The emotions and challenges are real.

However, as with a young child, if you put too much pressure on your young business to produce too much too quickly, you're going to miss what's really needed to make it strong.

If your business is new, you may have ideas about what it is, but you don't really know. The focus on play and experimentation means to not be attached to what the business looks like before it's had time to mature.

A client of ours was just starting out. Thankfully, he had not quit his job thinking his new business would just sprout. Instead, with enough financial security to breathe, he began to experiment and play with his business. Instead of it needing to produce immediately, he found a playfulness in himself and in the expression of his business, which came out in how he named his offers and in the language he used on his website. And that playfulness was fun! His audience started to build simply because of that energy.

And because he was playful, when he changed something because it didn't feel right to him, that was part of the playfulness. It didn't disrupt his business or upset his audience.

That kind of playfulness may not be your way, but it is helpful to hold what you do lightly as you try things out.

For this reason, the beginning is the wrong time to invest a lot of money and time in a fancy website, logo, branding, or anything like that. You have no idea yet what your business will look like as it moves through the developmental stages and becomes more successful. If you spend big on these kinds of things now, not only is it unnecessary, but chances are you'll just end up needing to redo it all in a year or so.

In fact, the client I mentioned above started out thinking that certain wording would resonate strongly with his chosen audience, but it took months to discover the actual language and wording that his best clients responded to. He was glad he hadn't spent much time or energy on branding and design at the early stage.

Heart of Business clients in the First Stage of development are always encouraged to focus exclusively on four elements. The more quickly they can become effective with these four, the sooner they start to see some financial results, and the sooner they can start to build more stability by working on the elements in the Second Stage.

The four elements are:

1. How to say what you do in a compelling way.

2. How to craft your first offer, including pricing, in a way that is resonant.

3. How to have an effective sales (or enrollment) conversation.

4. How to ask for referrals, which is the first and easiest step into marketing, reaching new people.

Let me explain what I mean by each element, then share some insights and cautions, too. You may find you need more in-depth learning on these. If so, that alone would be a lesson. All these elements are absolutely doable without your needing to be a marketing or business genius. Yet they do take some focus and some learning. They take leaning in and exploring things that may not be comfortable, or that you may have only seen done in shoddy or unethical ways.

So let's dig in to these four elements.

YOUR ONE COMPELLING SENTENCE

It's true, you do need to say what you do in an effective way. When people in business first start trying to say what they do, it often comes out vague, lengthy, or boring. It's stated in a way that glazes people's eyeballs over. It doesn't really engage anyone, and people end up drifting away. You want to be able to say what you do in a compelling way. I call this the *One Compelling Sentence.*

There are three crucial things you need to know about your One Compelling Sentence (OCS).

First, there is no magic phrase you can utter to a stranger so that they immediately say, "Oh wow, let me pay you!" I cover this in more detail in the later marketing chapters. But if you can take that in, it will hopefully bring in compassion and take the pressure off.

Second, you're not actually saying what you do. Instead, you're saying *who* you help, and *what* you help them with. This is what is known as "niching" or knowing your target market. It's the difference between me saying, "I use a strange blend of Sufi spiritual healing and business training, plus a variety of other communication and healing modalities I've learned over the years …," which puts everyone to sleep, versus me saying, "I love helping people in tiny businesses who want to make a difference in the world, who really need a business that works in a way that feels good to their heart."

The second way is much more compelling, and people get it. The first one is strange, wordy, and doesn't really work.

Third, almost everyone resists niching. They don't want to leave people out. They fear they won't reach enough people. They know what they do can help in many different situations and contexts.

Yet, from the thousands of clients with whom we've worked on this process, one of the most common comments we get is, "Ugh! I wish I hadn't resisted niching for so long. It makes everything easier, and it feels so good!" They find they are reaching the people that they are, in their hearts, *most* inspired to work with. They are often shocked and delighted that there are so many people in this very specific group. And they're having more fun and making more money than ever in their businesses.

This element, what we call the OCS, is the foundation of almost every other element throughout all the developmental stages. You don't have to get this perfect; there is no such thing as "perfect." But to arrive at enough clarity here to move forward, knowing that it will continue to evolve, means that all the other elements become *much* easier.

CRAFTING YOUR FIRST OFFER

Here's an open secret: people don't really want to buy what you're selling. What they want is to arrive somewhere.

One of our clients works with women in the second half of their lives who want and need to take control of their finances. Her clients don't want to buy sessions with her. Rather, what they want is to acquire knowledge and empowerment in relation to their finances, especially as retirement is not so far off anymore.

Crafting your offer, especially if you're a service provider, treads into the territory often termed "packages." Let me start by saying what packages are *not* about.

Packages are not discounts ("Buy six for the price of five!"). People are not buying your professional services the way they buy day-old bagels. They want and need the help. Of course people like to save money, but that's not the central reason they are deciding to work with you.

Neither are packages about forcing people to pay in big chunks. Clients can still pay in installments.

Here's what packages accomplish: they create a container of safety and care for your client so they feel carried toward the destination where they want to arrive.

When our boys were young and I was exhausted and sleep-deprived, I became extremely sick. My team and I at Heart of Business had been supporting a Portland, Oregon, holistic medicine clinic with their marketing, so I asked the owner for a recommendation. I ended up working with Jenny, a fantastic acupuncturist who supported my health for some years.

Following my first session, I asked her how soon I should come in. She told me what most small business owners/ practitioners say: "Well, just come in when you next need to." Because she and the rest of the clinic had been working with us, I was able to tell her, "No. What do you *really* want to tell me?"

Immediately she said, "I want you to come in weekly for the next month to six weeks and take the herbs I'm going to prescribe. Then, we'll probably be able to go to twice a month. I'm guessing in about three to four months your health will be built back up enough that you can come in once per month for maintenance."

A word about sovereignty, which we'll go into in more detail later. This acupuncturist clearly had sovereignty and experience in what she did. If you're new, you may not have yet developed that kind of certainty about what to do for clients, and that's okay. I want you to notice, however, the difference between being uncertain because you're learning, versus having the certainty but holding it back out of a false sense of wanting to give clients a choice.

She had no hesitation. She knew what I needed for the destination I wanted to reach: feeling healthy and vital again.

That is the essence of a package. It's a prescription, a full journey. By saying this to me and getting my commitment to this course of treatment, she helped me feel cared for, contained. She also then had a consistent client, which contributed to the stability of her business.

Often, practitioners don't want to make these kinds of recommendations because they want to empower their clients to make their own choices. Here's another open secret: if you withhold your recommendations for how your clients should work with you, they won't feel empowered; they'll feel abandoned.

That's the essence of crafting your offer. Ask yourself: Where does my client want to arrive? Where do I want them to arrive? What will it take to get them there? That can include number of sessions and frequency, as well as other things. With my acupuncturist, it was additional herbs. You might have other kinds of support to offer, such as meditation recordings, a workbook, or exercises. One client of ours ended up including a custom-crafted scent to help her clients relax. A realtor we know gave clients who bought a home one hour of time with a contractor.

After you pull that together, the final question is the price. What price feels good and resonant to *you*, if you're to provide what's needed for your client to arrive at their desired destination? When you see all you're providing and what the client gets at the end, it starts to feel more coherent and settled within you.

It's worth mentioning that pricing is a huge topic that people struggle with. We sometimes spend significant time with clients working through various emotional and business-related issues with setting a price that is accessible, ethical, sustainable, and profitable. The quick and clean version is to not get caught by the advice one hears so often to "charge what you're worth," which can be so entangling, or otherwise trying to charge top tier when you don't feel the confidence or clarity to do so.

Our approach is that you find a resonant price: one that feels good in your body. A simple exercise you can do, once you have an offer crafted, is to think of a price so low that you feel terrible charging it. Next step is to think of a price so high that you would freak out to charge that price. Finally, you allow yourself to move on a scale between those prices, noticing how different amounts land in your heart and your body.

When our clients do this kind of resonant pricing exercise, they rarely get just one price. Instead, they often get a significant amount of information, including the lowest price that feels acceptable, a price range where they feel more solid, and a higher price that may be for the future, once they gain more confidence and clarity.

I often counsel clients to not do two difficult things at the same time. This means that for those who have less client flow, it's fine to charge a lower price that still feels resonant just to get the flow going. For others, whose business is already robust and full, it may be time to stand solid with a higher price that really supports them.

Either way, I support you in making this difficult topic as approachable and ease-filled as possible.

SACRED SELLING

The third element of Stage One is what we call "Sacred Selling," which is the process of an ethical, focused sales conversation. When I got into business, I was surprised to find that I was actually pretty good at sales. I couldn't figure out why until I pulled apart the elements of selling.

I realized that focused, strategic, ethical sales involve three broad strokes.

The first has to do with the attitude of your heart. Because selling is the moment when a potential client says yes and pays you, a lot of neediness and grasping can arise in a business owner. It's not easy, but we teach our clients to have a healthy relationship with their own neediness. This allows them to be in a deep bow of service toward the client, and not have any energy of trying to "get" from them.

In chapter 2, I discussed how neediness is healthy and encouraged you to develop patience with it, to care for it. This is a great example of a moment in business when the neediness of the business owner, misdirected, can undermine an otherwise beautiful interaction. When you care for your own neediness first, you can hold a sincere attitude of service and care for the person who is considering spending money with you.

The second broad stroke is what we call compassionate questioning. Prior to Heart of Business, I had been a 911 paramedic for some years. I had gotten very good at assessments. I knew how to ask a bunch of questions with compassion and care, focus and intention. I knew how to find out what was going on and decide what was needed.

The essence, the heart, of a sales conversation is an assessment. Here, the business owner does not try to *get* the sale, but instead really tries to be in an attitude of curiosity and service. Your goal is to determine what's going on for the potential client and if you are the right person to help.

The third broad stroke combines dual intentions. On one hand, if it's true, you express your desire that, yes, you want to work with the client. They are invited and welcome. The second intention involves deeply honoring and respecting the client's sovereignty in making their own choices in their own time.

If you don't respect a client's sovereignty, it's easy to fall into manipulation, or hard sell. Here you try to force them to make the decision that you want, rather than the right decision for them. It's impossible to overstate how terrible manipulative sales are. They feel terrible in the heart to you as the seller. They of course feel terrible to the buyer, and they undermine, or often destroy entirely, any chance for long-term relationships or referrals.

At the same time, if you don't express to the client your desire to work with them, many will struggle to feel accepted, honored, and seen. They may in fact interpret your lack of invitation not as a way of giving them space to make a decision, but rather, as lack of care. I don't want to work with a professional who isn't genuinely interested in helping me, and your potential clients won't want to either.

ASKING FOR REFERRALS

Referrals are an essential aspect of your young business. I don't include other forms of marketing in Stage One. This is because, in early stages, reaching out to people you already know (those belonging to your existing social circles) is a much more direct way to go.

Of course, asking for referrals from your current network is rarely enough, but it's a great place to start. Remember, you're only on Stage One at this point. Except for the very few people who are natural connectors—those folks who naturally, seemingly without effort, create large networks of people—getting referrals can seem like an intimidating, mysterious process. Let me share two tips that will hopefully help you start to get your arms around the topic.

Anything you don't know how to do yet can seem intimidating, which is natural. With clarity about what's needed before you ask for a referral, and additional clarity on how to ask for a referral, it becomes much easier. It's even easier when you realize that you're asking for referrals from people who like you and want to support you.

First, put your One Compelling Sentence to use. Describe the kind of person you're trying to reach. There is a big difference between, "Hey, if you know anyone who could use me, please send them my way!" and "Hey, if you come across anyone who used to be really physically active, but now they're struggling with a chronic injury, I so want to help them."

That kind of clarity means the world to receiving effective referrals.

The second tip is to let the person you're asking know what happens after they send someone to you. People worry about pitching a friend into a hard-sell machine. If you can assure them, "I want you to know that anyone who reaches out, we start out with a short, no-pressure conversation, where I get a sense of whether I can help them or not. No pressure, and if I can't help, I may have a good referral for them."

These two pieces are key and can take you a long way in getting effective referrals.

As each of these four elements are put in place, a solidity begins to come into this First Stage of business. You know how to say what you do in a way that people respond to. You have a clear offer that you don't stumble over. You know how to be in service, in your heart, and focused in a sales conversation, so more people more easily become your clients. And you know how to ask for referrals, the beginning of having marketing in place that can stabilize the whole business.

You will get better with each, and cycle through them over time. But just making each minimally effective means it's time to focus on putting the Second Stage elements in place.

The Second Stage: Concentration

With the pieces from Stage One in place, it's time to amplify. The clarity you've achieved means you can begin to expand your reach. As you have more exploratory conversations with potential clients, a good number of them will become clients. Your schedule will start to fill up.

To get through Stage Two (Concentration) to Stage Three (Momentum), here are the four elements you need to focus on.

1. Clarifying and expanding your core message, which gets folded into your website.

2. Developing an effective website, which further clarifies how you are communicating your business and offers.

3. Creating consistent, compelling content, whether written, drawn, audio, or video.

4. Working on Heart-Centered Networking, which is an authenticity-based style of networking.

Your Core Message: The Customer-Focused Story

Let's begin by looking at what's involved in working on your core message. In Stage One, you created your One Compelling Sentence—a way of naming what you do and for whom you do it. But there needs to be more. There needs to be a deeper art and syntax to your core message.

By *syntax*, I mean an order for the different elements of a core message. When asked about the work they do, many business owners launch into a detailed, technical description of *how* they do their work. It's understandable. It seems like a natural answer to, "What do you do? How do you do that?"

Unfortunately, it's also often incredibly boring. Potential clients and visitors to your website don't want to know the technical aspects of your work. They are rarely interested in becoming a practitioner, like you. Their real questions are ones like, "Is this relevant to me? Is it going to be effective? Does it make sense? Is this person competent?"

By hearing the real questions, you can start to reply with what we call the Customer-Focused Story. It's based on what I call "marketing syntax." Syntax is how we organize words into comprehensible language. Take that sentence, for instance, and mess up the order of the words. "Comprehensible into words language organize syntax how is we." We can't understand that syntax, even though the words are all there, because they aren't in an understandable order. When you follow the rules of syntax, language becomes understandable.

"Marketing syntax" is understanding the order in which people need to hear things if they are to understand what you're telling them. Many marketing messages begin, "Here's your problem, and here's how to fix it." Or worse, "Here's this super cool thing you need." We turn away from those messages because they miss entire elements of syntax.

Without trying to teach the entire rules of marketing syntax, as we do in our Learning Community, I want to give you three general rules that will help you tremendously.

1. **First, start with empathy for the problem as they see it.** An acupuncturist may look at a patient and think, "They are wind deficient and their chi is low." But the patient is thinking, "Dang, I feel like complete crap, exhausted all the time." Empathy is speaking the language of the client. When you use their language, they feel seen and heard, which calms the nervous the system. It also lets them know that what you're saying is relevant to them.

2. **When you talk about what you do, talk in terms of the principles of your work, not the technical details or how-tos.** A principle is a statement of how the world works, from your point of view, not an action step. A client of mine who literally wrote the book on women's philanthropy identified the work's key principles and spoke about them with clients, readers, and others. People could immediately grasp why her approach was so powerful. For instance, one principle states, "Women bring more than money." That is a powerful truth, rather than a complicated how-to that might bore people.

3. **Remember that you're not trying to convince them of anything.** Be brief, and if they are interested, they can ask for more information: "Tell me more about that!" That's a good thing! It doesn't mean you failed

in communicating, it means you've succeeded in engaging with someone.

A client of ours, starting with the One Compelling Sentence, then wrote her full Customer-Focused Story. She shared it with a friend who had known her and her work for years. The friend said, "I love this new focus you have! It's so clear, I immediately get it!" Our client confided to her friend that that's what she's been doing with clients for over a decade. It wasn't new, it was just suddenly extremely clear.

The lack of clarity is really common. When your core message becomes this clear and powerful, it has a tremendous impact on your whole business. One of the first things we use it for is to rapidly and easily create your website content, which is the second element.

Your Website

The second element of Concentration involves creating an effective, compelling, heart-centered website and developing a strategy around how to use your website so you can start to amplify your reach.

Your website is meant to be a way for folks to check out you and your work from a distance, with safety. If you follow marketing syntax and are also vulnerable and authentic on your website, then, if your work is for them, people who visit your website will feel seen and safe.

There are three kinds of visitors to your website, each with a different purpose. There are new people, who want to get a sense of whether what you do is relevant to their situation and whether they trust and like you. You are *not* trying to immediately sell these folks on your services. The assumption that you're trying to get someone to buy immediately creates a lot of pain and manipulation in marketing. You don't have to do that. Chapter 7 goes into a lot more detail about this dynamic, but for right now, know that you are just starting the process of building a relationship with someone new.

A second kind of visitor is someone who already knows you and is looking to register/enroll/sign up. Because these folks are very often already in relationship with you, they are coming to your website from a link in an email, social media, or by some other direct means. Often, these visitors head straight to the offer that is relevant to them.

A third kind of visitor is a current client or customer who is trying to access resources through your site. At Heart of Business, we have all kinds of resources for our clients, and they access those in a special section of our website.

By understanding these three main kinds of visitors and how they end up on your website, you can see that your main pages need to be focused on creating a relationship of trust, safety, and connection with new people. The other two kinds of visitors already know where they are going. Sure, you want the links that those visitors need to be clear and findable, but they don't need to be front and center.

Our clients have found that by using the marketing syntax laid out in the Customer-Focused Story and creating website content, they often hear from folks, "I felt like you totally get me! I felt so much trust in you just from reading your website." That's what you want: a website that can represent you and your work and engage with people when you can't be there personally.

Your Content

Let me speak to the resistance many feel when they consider creating content—e.g., articles, audio, video—for an audience. First, it can feel incredibly vulnerable to put your voice out into the world. Also, there is a sense that the world is already overwhelmed with too much content.

"People have already said this. I'm not adding anything unique," you might think. This fear of having nothing new to say is common. Many still believe you must be a "star creator" with thousands or millions of followers if you are going to offer content.

The rise of technology (like the printing press), followed by widespread literacy then broadcast technology, means that for that last eighty to one hundred years, relatively few people have been considered "star talent" creators, with hundreds of millions of people receiving content from them. The rest of us were just supposed to consume that content.

I reject this model. For most of human history, communication was in much smaller groups. Even "stars" didn't have millions of followers; there just wasn't the technology to reach those people.

The rise of the internet and the ability for anyone to create and publish content disrupted the monopoly of these star creators. Instead, we've returned in many ways to what was normal: smaller groups of people communicating with each other. Let go of the need to be a "star talent."

Instead, embrace the truth that there are quite a few people out there who could really benefit from being in conversation with you—yes you—about the topic you're uniquely poised to help them with. Many other people may have said countless things on this topic. But there's something about who *you* are that enables your audience to hear it in a way that will make a difference to them.

We talk about this in terms of your Jewel, which I talk about in more detail in chapter 9, in combination with your personality, or who you are. With your unique presence, and offering a more intimate, accessible space for content delivery, you are providing something invaluable to your clients. It's one thing to read a published book or follow a well-known personality. It's another to be on the email list of someone who reads and replies to their emails or comments on social media.

One of our clients embraced this, despite strong resistance and feelings of vulnerability. She started tentatively putting some content out there, taking a risk and showing her heart, expressing what was important to her, and showing care for the people in her audience. Because she did it on the foundation of clarity from the earlier elements she'd developed, her audience responded in ways that surprised her, expressing appreciation and sharing her articles with friends.

Even though many books had already been written in her field, her voice, her empathy, her willingness to show up, and her ability to make her audience feel like they knew her all helped the content land with much more impact than she could have guessed.

So yes, you might be saying what's already been said. But your more human-sized audience needs to hear it, often many times, and likely they can hear it better coming from you. Despite the multitude of gardening and homesteading books out there, I read the newsletter and watch videos from someone I knew in Ithaca, New York, whose voice and approach I really like. Your content will play that role for folks in your audience.

Your heart, your presence, is important. From the Sufi perspective, there is a Unity of Oneness. Everything is part of the whole. If anything is missing, then we are not whole. If your heart is missing, if you are missing, then we are not whole.

The next thing to bear in mind about content creation is this: you can learn how to create compelling content without losing your own authentic voice. You don't need to copy any particular person, but you can take inspiration from people who express themselves in ways that resonate with you. That's the gift of there being so many creators. Some people love writing longer, more nuanced pieces. Others like writing concise and inspiring pieces. Others prefer video. Still others prefer audio. Some prefer drawing.

I have a friend and colleague who has developed a way of communicating he calls "dharma doodles." They are comic-style drawings that express profound truths in accessible ways. Another creator, one of our clients and a facilitator in our Learning Community, makes videos on trauma healing rather than writing about this subject.

There are so many ways forward. Whatever modality best suits you, your content items like videos, drawings, newsletters, and blog articles are crucial. Why? Because they allow people to feel seen, get help, and get a sense of who you are—and all this *before* they need to be vulnerable by connecting directly with you.

HEART-CENTERED NETWORKING

A customer-focused story, an effective website, and compelling content work together to allow you to expand your reach into new audiences through heart-centered networking. You aren't necessarily trying to gain ten thousand or one hundred thousand followers (although, you might get there). For the most part, microbusinesses can do well when they have a few hundred to a few thousand in their audience.

There are several things that make the task of reaching new people easier.

First, place your primary focus on relationships. For instance, you will be a lot more effective sharing your content with a handful of people who each have a handful of friends or community, than trying to automate some "scaling" process of advertising to thousands.

In the First Stage, you learned about asking for referrals. Networking keeps that focus and expands it beyond your closest circles. It's much easier to ask people to connect you with folks who need help, rather than asking them, "Do you want to hire me?" By asking for referrals, especially those who might want your content, you minimize pressure because you're not trying to sell to someone you don't yet know. Most people feel a sense of openness to support someone who is wanting to help others.

If you approach others with vulnerability, sincerity, and love, it shows. People can feel authenticity. Let your heart-centered networking efforts sound something like this: "I see many [x] kinds of people struggling with [y], and I really want to reach them. Do you know folks like that?"

If someone in your audience connects with what you're saying, they'll raise their hand and say, "That's me!" Otherwise, they are often happy to help spread the word.

Now, if you identify as introverted, sensitive, or just shy, it can be difficult to network—even if you're doing it in a relational, sincere way. You might even think you simply can't take this step. You're not alone.

It helps to bear in mind that there are so many ways to develop networking relationships. You can reach out in a way that benefits both your business and those you want to help. And there is *no* reason to do it in a way that doesn't feel congruent with who you are.

A client of ours, who identified as extremely introverted, had been invited to give a talk on her topic to a relatively small group—about twelve to sixteen people—in a clinic. She struggled with this, but we embraced the truth of how she liked to move in the world.

Instead of a talk, she offered to make herself available for short, one-on-one conversations. The person who invited her said that sounded great, so she circulated a sign-up sheet for people to have individual conversations with her. She had fewer people than would have been in the room, maybe eight instead of sixteen. But she also had much deeper connections to each of those people and ended up gaining clients from that experience.

You can make your business visible to new people in ways that feel good to your heart.

Putting these four elements in place means that your business will start to feel even more solid, like it's an actual business! There are other elements that end up getting put into place in the Second Stage as well, making for a really robust business. I go into more detail in chapter 9, where I explain some of the other pieces that help fill out your business, and even more detail in the appendix. But these four elements are the central, fundamental pieces needed.

As you progress through the Second Stage, your business will most likely start making real money, and you'll be able to see the light at the end of the tunnel: that the business can actually support you.

At the same time, these two early stages of business development can sometimes feel challenging, because you already want the business to be flying. It's okay. Slowing down, having compassion for yourself, and realizing you don't have to get it all done at once means that you can focus on one element at a time. This will move you faster and more efficiently in surprising ways.

Also, as you build the outer structures and engage with more clients, you will naturally be strengthening your heart connection as well. Building a heart-centered business is a spiritual journey.

Things to Remember:
- Have compassion for yourself and your business. It's not broken, it's developing. It's okay to slow down and put the pieces in place step by step.
- In the early stages, do things simply and cheaply; don't invest a lot of money or time in fancy branding or marketing. Chances are you'll have to redo it all as you learn more about your business.
- The First Stage is just learning to walk, with a focus on play and experimentation. It's learning how to say what you do in a compelling way, craft a clear offer, become comfortable and effective with the sales conversation, and learn how to ask for referrals so you can start the flow in your business.
- The Second Stage is about expanding your reach on the strength of the First Stage. Developing a more in-depth message, crafting a website and other content, then expanding your marketing beyond those you know already means you can start to feel lift under your wings!
- For each element you put in place, you're going for "minimally effective," not perfect. Over time you will return to each element, making them better and better as you learn more about your business.

CHAPTER 5

Stages Three and Four and the Maturing Business

Stage Two (Concentration) is exciting because the business feels like it's really working. As you progress through this stage, there are months where you make enough money and have a sense of flow in your business. However, it's still not quite Momentum (Stage Three), and this is because of the "feast-or-famine" dynamic that shows up in late Concentration.

I observed this dynamic happening regularly for most people in mid-to-late Stage Two, and the reasons are obvious. When someone puts all the pieces in place from Stage One and Two, things begin to work. The marketing works, sacred selling works, and the business has clients. But what also happens is that their capacity is filled with paying clients. They find themselves too busy to maintain the elements they have put in place to that point, such as marketing and networking.

Then, quite organically, clients complete and move on. The business owner soon finds they no longer have enough clients. However, what they do have is more time, so they lean back into the things they did that made them busy in the first place. But it's not like a faucet that can be turned on to create an instant flow; often, there's a lag time before clients start showing up again.

That lag time is where the "famine" part comes in. Then, after working on the business for a while, a new wave of paying clients arrives, and the business owner's schedule fills up. The cycle repeats.

To step out of this cycle, you need to move into the Third Stage by putting some key elements in place.

The Third Stage: Momentum

I define Momentum as the stage where you can fully trust your business. All elements of your business are working. You're making plenty of money. Even when your business is in "low tide" and your numbers are lower, they are still higher than what you need to be profitable.

The four elements that help a business move from Stage Two to Stage Three are these:

- Establish core systems.
- Get just enough support (not necessarily anyone on payroll, although that's sometimes true).
- Implement more sophisticated marketing.
- Create a garden path of offers.

ESTABLISH CORE SYSTEMS

Many of us have had terrible experiences with business systems, whether they entail "customer service representatives" who only follow a script and can't actually help you; online bots; or rigid policies that protect the company but aren't helping the customers.

I want to invite you to think of systems differently. Our own bodies are, in fact, comprised of systems. Some of them function consciously, such as when we reach with our hand to pick up something we need. Others function unconsciously, such as our respiratory system. At rest, human adults take twelve to sixteen breaths per minute, bringing in oxygen that fuels our cells while simultaneously offloading carbon dioxide and other waste—all this below the level of conscious thought.

Your business has a "beingness" to it—a heart of its own, as I've explained. One of the ways this heart manifests is when the business does things without you.

Here are some examples:

- When your website creates a connection with a new visitor and they feel enough trust to give their email address. A system delivers this new subscriber something that you created, which helps them.

- When a receipt email comes in and is forwarded automatically to a bookkeeping service, which enters it as an expense.

- When a client can access, again through your website, resources that support them—say, a recording of a guided meditation—without you needing to send anything to them.

In addition, there are systems that involve you but remove your need to think about it. Things like checklists and workflows are systems. Decision-making, or any kind of thinking, uses up a surprising amount of energy. There is a theory that our brains evolved from around 300 cubic centimeters in size to around 1,500 cubic centimeters—a fivefold growth—after we discovered how to use fire to cook food. Cooking food makes a *lot* more calories available, which allowed a calorie- and blood-intensive organ like the brain to grow.

Even if you're involved in doing tasks, by implementing systems like checklists and workflows, you reduce the amount of thinking required, which frees up energy and creativity for other tasks that really need it.

Here's an example of a workflow/checklist system. Say you want to send clients cards on their birthdays. You establish an online enrollment system wherein the client's address is added into a contact manager; their birthday is automatically entered into your calendar; and an alarm is set for two weeks prior to the client's birthday. In addition, a regular reminder in your task list prompts you to buy envelopes, cards, and stamps on a regular basis.

When the birthday reminder pops up, you have the card and materials at hand to wish them a happy birthday. And maybe you'll even find your note is written with a bit more care and heart-presence, because you didn't have to waste mental energy worrying you'd forget it or run out of postage.

GET JUST ENOUGH HELP

Systems can only take you so far. Even the most efficient and productive systems require maintenance and engagement, and it's rare that a business can function in Momentum without any additional help from people beyond the business owner.

I want to be clear that I am not necessarily talking about payroll. My own company does have a small payroll, but many self-employed or otherwise "solo" businesses don't have a payroll at all. Instead, they've hired other self-employed folks, or small businesses, with specific skills. As a business owner, you are more likely to be thought of as their client rather than their boss.

For instance, I had a client who was exhausted and overwhelmed, trying to get beyond income limits in the mid-five figures (US dollars). They had put systems in place, their offers were compelling, and they had clients; however, there were limits they just couldn't get past. Tasks like bookkeeping, solving tech problems, and posting online content were sapping time and energy. This client felt bogged down in logistical activities and unable to push the business forward in more inspired, powerful directions.

The business income was low enough that that the thought of hiring help felt risky to this client. However, they checked in with their heart, took a deep breath, and decided to take my advice to get the help. They hired a bookkeeper for one to two hours per month; a web-support person to handle online tech issues for one to two hours per month; and a virtual assistant who helped with a variety of client support and small tasks (like getting articles and videos published and posted) for ten hours per month.

Although they totaled only fourteen hours per month (about three hours per week), these supports opened more client slots, which more than paid for the help. Most importantly, my client had time and space to dream once again: about the business, their goals, and their visions. Things began to move forward in powerful new ways. Suddenly, the business had new life and began to thrive and grow—all without payroll or a huge monetary investment.

IMPLEMENT MORE SOPHISTICATED MARKETING

I want to be clear that "more sophisticated" doesn't necessarily mean more complicated or more expensive.

We'll be talking a lot more about marketing in chapters 6 and 7. We'll cover what marketing is (and is not), marketing's true purpose, and how to be in healthy relationship with it.

For now, suffice it to say that moving into Momentum requires more thoughtful, less haphazard marketing than earlier stages. For instance, it might require marketing more consistently across multiple platforms, or nurturing partnerships and collaborations to support growth and expand your reach. These are just a few examples.

In any event, "more sophisticated" means that your business has systems and help that ensure that your marketing still has a tremendous amount of heart, care, and connection—even as it's consistently reaching more people. Additionally, more sophisticated marketing means your business is not disrupted or waylaid when you become busy with clients and other deliverables.

CREATE A GARDEN PATH OF OFFERS

Broadly speaking, there are two ways for a business to bring in more money: sell more of one thing to new people, or sell new things to current and past clients and customers.

At Heart of Business, we use the term "garden path" instead of what many people call the "funnel." This is because we find the concept of a funnel incredibly inaccurate. For one, it feels underhanded and unethical to have the mindset that you are forcing people into a tighter and tighter path. Unfortunately, all too often, this is precisely the goal when manipulative, high-pressure sales techniques are at play.

What's more, the concept of a funnel is based on the idea that first someone buys a low-priced item, followed by a mid-priced item, followed by a premium-priced item. Andrea J. Lee, the noted business coach and author of *Pink Spoons*, was the first person I heard challenge this idea—and rightly so.

When I myself observed how our clients were acting, I too saw that it just didn't bear out. Some Heart of Business clients come in at a more reserved spending level, perhaps spending a few hundred dollars on a course, and maybe the same amount on another course later on. Other clients never take a course at that level, but step directly into premium-priced individual coaching. Of course, some people do go through the low price, medium price, premium price sequence, but it's by no means universal.

When a business has more than one offer, it is helpful to think about it like a garden path. A garden needs an entrance, where most people come in. But then there are choices (or paths). Sometimes there aren't a lot of choices, because a small business can't easily make more than a small handful of offers. But still, there are options.

How do you know it's time to start thinking about changes to the business model you're using, to begin to create a garden-path structure? When you find yourself hitting ceilings around income and capacity, without being able to make the money you want and need to make, it might be time.

For instance, a client of ours was doing decently well, making around sixty thousand dollars (US) per year while in Stage Two. That is nothing to sniff at, obviously, and lots of people would be happy to see their business generating that much. However, in reality, it's not enough to pay for business expenses as well as pay the business owner enough to care for kids, save for retirement, cover household expenses, and accomplish other personal financial goals.

But for this client the ceiling was real. She found herself unable to make much more without either raising her rates to levels that didn't feel healthy to her or working more hours than were sustainable.

That's a business model problem. Solving it required introducing some new offers, including offers to groups, that enabled her to bring in a bit more money with less time, while still maintaining integrity in her work. But it also required more sophisticated thinking about other kinds of courses and offers that could lift her income to the ninety thousand dollars per year she really wanted to be making without overtaxing her time or energy reserves.

At Heart of Business, we helped her transition to offering several groups a larger course, with fewer one-on-one client sessions. A large part of what made this possible was the implementation of more sophisticated, consistent marketing. Our client expanded her audience in significant ways—ways that allowed her to enroll larger courses and keep her groups full.

A year later, the end result was that she was making more than her target income without putting in more time and energy—and without giving an inch of her ethical high ground.

So by engaging these four elements (establishing core systems, getting just enough help, instituting more sophisticated marketing, and creating a garden path), your business can gain real Momentum. That is, it can become more stable, sustainable, and profitable. You'll find yourself solidifying and even expanding the gains made in the first two stages of business development.

Because the Stage Three elements are so stabilizing, they allow the business to be in clear Momentum. All the needs of the business are being handled, the owner isn't overworked, and income needs are being met or exceeded. This is when it's really fun.

Most of our clients are content to stop here, either for a little while or permanently, and enjoy the fun and ease!

For those inspired and heart-guided to go further, there is a Fourth Stage. It's entirely optional. You should know about it so that you can decide if you want to work toward it. Or, perhaps even more importantly, if you want to ignore pressure from others saying you should "go for it" when you don't really want to.

The Fourth Stage: Independence

Up until you now, you have gained more independence in your life as your business runs more easily and becomes more stable and profitable. We call the Fourth Stage Independence because the focus is now helping *the business itself* gain independence: you work to make the business able to function well without you present. Whether you want to sell the business, take a long sabbatical, or just have a larger business that doesn't weigh you down, Stage Four elements are what help your business become independent from your constant presence.

When someone tells me they want to get to the Fourth Stage, I always push back. For most microbusiness owners, what they are really looking for is a high-functioning, stable, profitable Stage Three business in Momentum. Businesses in true Momentum still allow the owner to take vacations or other breaks and be able to afford it. Honestly, most business owners are happy at that level.

Stage Four happens when there are others in your business who can do the work that you do with clients, without you. There's a team that can run the business, and you can ultimately be replaced if you want.

The benefits of this stage are several. First, the business can generate revenue even if you take a long sabbatical. That is, it can essentially run without you. It can also, often, scale to be impactful for many more people than you, by yourself, could ever reach alone. As well, the business can be sold or otherwise handed down (or over) to others.

It can be exciting.

The reason I push back, however, is that this stage requires that you take on an entirely different job: that of becoming a CEO. It requires surrender and letting go so others can step in. It requires significant resources, and the investment in systems and team very often comes before the business scales up enough to cover those costs.

It often requires you, as the business owner, to give attention to this process for several years. This means you won't be as involved in working directly with clients during that time.

The risks of moving into Stage Four can be significant. You might never catch up with the cycle of cost. You might hit ceilings of growth that, for a variety of reasons, you cannot get past. You might end up personally making about as much money as you were making with a well-developed Stage Three business—or perhaps less. It often requires getting to a certain scale to make the move to Stage Four worthwhile. For instance, having one practitioner working under you with clients often doesn't expand your business capacity enough to make it worthwhile. You may need five or ten practitioners to account for the additional time and resources it takes to support them.

Here are the four elements that are needed to make the leap into Stage Four: Independence.

- **Evolve a Business Model** that works at a significantly larger scale.
- **Develop Delivery of Services** that doesn't require you.
- **Hire and Lead a Team** who have their full focus on the business.

- **Expand Your Marketing Scale**, so your scaled business model is filled up.

Evolve a Business Model

The business model already made an appearance in Stage Three. Here, the business model needs to evolve again. Because a Stage Four business has more expenses, the business model needs to be able to bring in the revenue to cover those expenses, and it's unlikely that your Stage Three model, where the business owner is still delivering all the services, is going to be able to generate revenue at that level.

This is where you see scaled offers like membership sites; having practitioners who work with clients or groups; or other models that allow for scale.

This kind of scaling can obviously be done; lots of people have. But it takes attention, care, love, and resources to do it well, without losing the quality and impact you brought yourself as the business owner.

Develop Delivery of Services That Doesn't Require You

This element is intimately linked to the business model but is something different. If you are going to use other people to deliver your services, you'll have to decide how they'll be trained. Most choose to have practitioners come with some recognized basic training certificate from their field, then further train or mentor them in their business's particular approach. Once they are trained, some time and effort goes into making sure these practictioners are performing well with your clients.

Alternatively, some use do-it-yourself models, such as home-study programs or learning modules, where clients can work through learning or development on their own. This requires testing and development to ensure your clients are getting good results without the handholding of working with someone personally.

Most often, there is a hybrid model, where practitioners use materials the owner has developed to walk clients through whatever services are offered.

In some industries, this is easier, where practitioners come trained: for instance, a holistic health clinic, where every practitioner has already been trained and earned a certificate or license in their modality. In other professions or businesses, where the owner has developed their own work, at least some of that training and mentoring needs to be developed and provided by the owner.

Hire and Lead a Team

At this stage it's nearly impossible to avoid having employees on an actual payroll. The scale of the business and the needs of operations require people to be focused on the business as their primary work concern.

Previously, the business owner has often gotten by through hiring professionals who are themselves business owners. Web developers, virtual assistants, and accountants are all self-employed with their own businesses; you are really their client, not their boss.

Here, you need to learn how to hire actual employees. Hiring, onboarding, delegating, and leading are all separate skills and processes that require a lot of learning if you haven't done them before. Making mistakes here is inevitable because we're all human, and these mistakes tend to be way more expensive than those made in earlier stages.

You can still move relatively slowly, hiring just one person at a time, as you learn and grow. But your vision, and the needs of the business, may push you faster than you're comfortable with.

The learning curve can be steep, and yet it can feel amazing to have a skilled, inspired, collaborative team in place that really cares.

Expand Your Marketing Scale

Needless to say, all this requires a lot more clients and buyers to fill up your business model and generate the revenue to pay all the expenses—including, hopefully, more to you as well for all this work.

This, in turn, requires scaling up your marketing and your sales processes significantly. You will need people on your team to help handle marketing and sales, so they can be effective while you are leading the whole enterprise.

You're really becoming a CEO, and you're learning that leaders do a lot of work—and they must do it well—or the whole business can struggle.

It Looks Different for Different Businesses

Some people find that their business needs a team of twenty to function in really powerful ways. Others work much more minimally, perhaps with a core team of five people and a double handful of contracted practitioners to help deliver to clients.

My friend and colleague Les McKeown, who has a ton of experience in this arena, wrote an incredible book called *Predictable Success*. McKeown's book talks specifically about how companies with teams get to a stable place. If you are headed in the direction of Independence, *Predictable Success* will give you many insights into what will be needed to make your team-based business work.

I have really enjoyed coaching business owners who are taking on Stage Four. But they must be clear in their own hearts that this is what they truly want. It starts with asking some specific questions once your business is settling into Stage Three.

Stage Four Discernment: Six Questions

A Heart of Business Learning Community member was telling me about the rush of clients she'd had with the onset of the COVID-19 pandemic. She wanted to hire a friend and colleague, a professional who does the same work she does, to work with her clients.

This is, in some ways, the essence of what Stage Four is about: having someone else work with your clients.

But the way our client was talking about it raised flags for me. There are questions that need to be asked and answered honestly before you bring someone on and start down the path to creating a Stage Four business. Why? Because if you bring someone on without really looking at the issues involved, you can sink your business.

First question: Do you really have the consistent, ongoing client flow to justify it?

Due to the pandemic, our client, who does financial coaching, had a rush of new clients that overwhelmed her initially. Which is fantastic! The issue here is that that rush came due to world events rather than her own marketing efforts, which she admitted were not very robust.

Because her own marketing had not invited in that rush of clients, there was no way she could confidently predict it would continue. What's more, even though the number of clients was a high watermark for her, and more than she could handle personally in any moment, it wasn't enough to keep another person fully busy.

If your own marketing isn't consistently bringing in a tremendous excess of business, then you may be overextending yourself to bring someone else on.

Second question: Do you have to train new people in your methodology?

Our client, over the course of many years, had developed her own methodology specific to her business. Anyone working for her needed to be trained in that methodology at a high level if they were to provide it as a practitioner. This would take months of initial training, plus ongoing oversight and mentoring. For someone already overwhelmed, that can wipe you out.

Additionally, ask yourself, do you know *how* to train someone in your approach? Do you know how to evaluate them to determine when they know enough to work with your clients, representing your business and reputation? And, as importantly, can you do it without neglecting other important parts of your business?

Third question: Are you ready to invest in legal, financial, and administrative structures?

Bringing on other practitioners requires legal contracts, awareness of employment law in your area, different accounting structures, payroll (or at least ways of paying contractors), and tracking systems for it all.

It's a significant investment and setup. It takes not only money but your precious time.

Fourth question: Does your pricing/business model support having others working under you?

All this added overhead and time needs to be accounted for somehow. Industry standards for coaching or other similar professional services pay between 25 and 40 percent of client fees to a contracted practitioner. The other 60 to 75 percent helps the business pay for infrastructure, time, administration, marketing, and accounting, and still have some profit.

This, unfortunately, means the coaching fees need to be significant enough to pay decently. If you're charging one hundred dollars (US) per session currently, you can see how that might not really work for the contractor or the business.

Fifth question: Do you have enough client demand to justify bringing on not just one, but several practitioners?

Because of the significant costs, infrastructure, and time that it takes to manage practitioners well, it's often not worth it to add just one additional practitioner. It's often better if you have at least two or three. That way, you can pay them decently while covering your costs and still making a profit.

That means having enough clients to keep you, plus two or three practitioners, busy enough. Perhaps your practitioners would not be earning a full-time income, but they would be doing enough work with clients to stay interested, and to deem the investment of time and effort worth their while.

Sixth question: Why do you really want to do this?

While the *why* question is often a good place to start, I often ask it last in this context. Here, it helps to see the why after really understanding what's involved.

The two most common reasons I hear are: "I want to help a friend" and "I don't want to work on my own, I want someone else around."

After answering the first five questions, you will know better whether trying to help a friend in this way might, in fact, end up sinking your business. And if you are feeling alone in the business, there are other ways to get your needs for cameraderie met. For example, you can create a mastermind group with peers, colleagues, or just other heart-centered business owners. You can hire a coach or join a business community. Or you can develop a network of peer/colleague relationships, people you can call to talk to regularly.

One of the better answers to this sixth question—one that tells me perhaps the client is right to want to expand in this way—is something along these lines: "I've been building up my marketing and client base to the point where I always have a waiting list, and we have a large audience. I want to serve many more people who really need our help, and I'm really interested in learning how to help others work with our clients and do it well."

If your answers to the above six questions show you that perhaps taking on practitioners is not something you want to do right now, here are a few alternatives:

- **Create a waiting list.** That can be a wonderful feeling.
- **Raise your prices.** A waiting list with a lot of eager clients who want to work with you specifically is one of the signs that your prices could go up.
- **Experiment with different models.** Do you run any groups? Have you created any programs? What can you do to serve a larger number of people without taking more of your time?
- **If you're wanting to help a friend and can do it, refer clients to them.** Rather than bring them into your business, send them referrals for their own business.
- **Enjoy the heck out of your situation!** If you're in a place like our client was with an abundance of work, then instead of always wanting to expand and grow, sometimes you can just sit back and enjoy the fruits of the situation.

Taking on a practitioner, and thereby starting to move your business into Stage Four, is a huge endeavor. It can affect your business and your time in big ways. Make sure you think through the factors, check with your heart, and take your time before setting out on that path. It can be an amazing journey to have others working in your business like this! Or it can be a disaster if you're not ready for it.

Where Is Your Business?

The intention of this developmental model is to bring compassion, focus, and clarity to your efforts to grow your business. I'm inviting you right now to sit with what you've learned in this chapter and the previous one, using it as a gentle lens on your own business.

Using the elements from the different stages, discern for yourself what stage your business is in. As you do this, be kind. Remember that you're not looking for perfection from each element—just that any element that *is* in place is there enough to be effective.

This developmental model is not taught universally, so most people, perhaps including you, have started developing their business in a more hodgepodge fashion. Because of this, most businesses have elements from multiple stages: two or three from Stage One, one or two from Stage Two, maybe even something from Stage Three. This is normal.

Our clients have found it easiest, and most helpful and effective, to consider themselves in the lowest stage with missing elements. Commonly I see businesses that have quite a bit of Stage Two put into place, including a website, a regular newsletter, and a social media presence, plus some other attempts at marketing. Yet they are struggling badly because they aren't clear on their audience, their offer is muddy, and they lack confidence in the sales conversation.

By focusing on the lowest stage that still has missing or incomplete elements, the business gains traction most quickly. So in the example above, despite all that is in place from Stage Two, we would consider a business like this in Stage One: Creation.

The good news is that once the Stage One elements are implemented, and the already present Stage Two elements are tweaked to be in alignment with Stage One, *boom*: big things can happen quickly.

With this developmental model understood, let's bring some love and, yes, healing, into one of the most painful topics for small business owners: marketing.

Things to Remember:
- Your business isn't broken, it's developing. Embracing where your business is in the developmental model enables you to focus, prioritize, and relax.
- The goal is effectiveness, not perfection. All these elements will evolve and change with time, and they often need to be worked with several times before they really shine. Get each element minimally effective, then move on to the next.
- Focus on the lowest stage with missing elements. Avoid the temptation to jump ahead just because someone said you "should."

- Most business owners are looking for a well-functioning Stage Three business. Take real care and be honest with yourself before taking on the journey into Stage Four.
- Be kind to yourself. The journey from Stage One to Stage Three usually takes two to four years of focus on development. The journey from Stage Three to Stage Four takes another two to three years or more.

CHAPTER 6

The True Purpose of Marketing

I f you dislike, distrust, or just plain hate marketing—or if you have reactions to being asked to market your business—you've probably been told that you need to "get over" those reactions. In other words, push through, put on your big kid pants, and do the thing anyway.

If that's you, I want you to hear what I have to say. You've heard this next piece from me before, and now, in this context, I want you to pause and let this next sentence really sink in.

Your heart is sensing something true, and your reaction has wisdom in it.

This is critical. I said it about business in general, I said it about money, and now the spotlight is on marketing. Your heart is your best navigator in business and in the world in general. Trusting your heart will help you navigate the many challenges that come up. There are excellent reasons you have for reactions to marketing, and it's your heart's integrity that keeps you from following through with acting.

Or, if you are acting, it has you cringing and no doubt holding back or otherwise doing it less than wholeheartedly.

Again, I'm going to ask you to trust your heart—and also to lean in. It's your heart's wisdom keeping you from following through with painful or unethical marketing strategies. It is also true that people need to hear from you. Leaning in means finding a way through to a new relationship, this time with marketing—one that allows you to fully embrace your heart, yet still show up in ways that feel good.

To get there, I want to offer a brief history of unethical marketing. Deepening your awareness of these origins will help you understand your justifiable reactions. I also want to name some of the most common unethical sales tactics. That way, you can see them for what they are, which will help you make sense of why they feel so bad.

After considering the stories and schemes of unethical marketing, I'll explain what I see as marketing's true purpose. Most importantly, I'll show you how you can be in a healthier relationship with marketing. This will prepare you for the next chapter on the Three Journeys of Marketing.

A (Very) Brief History of Unethical Marketing

In the early 1900s, during the infancy of modern psychology, early psychologists like John Watson and Walter Scott used their understanding of the human mind and behavior to help advertising executives sell products. John Watson, who worked for advertising agency J. Walter Thompson, eventually become a vice-president at Thompson's agency.

Watson created and executed high-profile ad campaigns for personal care products (among others).

Watson (and others like him) believed inciting and stoking human fear, anger, greed, and addiction was the best way to sell things. His advertising advice included quotes like this: "[T]ell him [that is, the consumer] something that will tie him up with fear, something that will stir up a mild rage, that will call out an affectionate or love response, or strike a deep psychological or habit need." In other words, market your products by activating people's deepest emotional responses, which has them reacting unconsciously by buying.

John Watson was not the only psychologist partnering with advertisers in this way. Many early academics of the relatively new discipline of psychology turned their findings to the field of advertising, gaining positions in the new Madison Avenue advertising agencies during the 1930s and beyond.

The early twentieth century marriage of psychology and marketing produced ethically problematic approaches that have been used over and over since. It became standard, for example, to include product placements in children's stories, so that today we see entire shows centered on children's toys. The tobacco industry used fake science to resist efforts to make public the link between smoking and cancer. The oil industry followed suit, attempting to refute the overwhelming evidence that carbon is related to climate change. It's no wonder people like you and me who really care about the world are beyond skeptical about marketing.

There is a lot more history that could be discussed. For now, it's enough to simply point out how twentieth century academics and advertisers partnered together to hone and perfect the art of mass human manipulation for the sole purpose of profit, and how this was done without concern for any harm (individual, social, environmental) that might result.

The effects of this history are ongoing and deeply grievous. We are all profoundly justified in being skeptical and resistant to anything called "marketing."

Terrible Marketing Tactics: An Overview

There are, of course, many ways marketing is done terribly. As well, there are many ways it can be done in a beautiful, caring fashion. I always find it helpful to know why something is terrible, rather than to just have a vague gut feeling. When I know specifics, then I don't have to try to talk myself out of my feelings. Then, in searching for more beautiful ways to do something, I know specifically what to avoid.

Outright lying tops the list of terrible marketing tactics, of course. Petroleum companies, cigarette companies, and many other large corporations have done just this.

It's best to avoid lying. I say that somewhat glibly. Yet I really mean it.

Years ago, I got caught up in a network-based, multi-level marketing company. In this dysfunctional business model, individual sellers recruit others to also sell for them. This particular company encouraged those of us selling the products to omit the truth, which is one form of lying. We were told explicitly, "Tell everyone the success stories, but only tell your upline (that is, those above you in the sponsorship structure) about the problems, failures, and complaints."

Now, it's natural enough in any business to want to talk about how well it works, and to avoid amplifying the things that inevitably go wrong. However, in this instance, the hush policy around problems was very strict. You would immediately lose support and sponsorship if you ever said anything negative.

I remember vividly when my wife Holly hit her limit around the company's lack of integrity. "Mark. This is no good." She was right. The company insisted their products were 100-percent good for everyone, no exceptions. They also claimed everyone selling the products would reach a certain distributor level. Yet, when I sat down and worked out the numbers reflected by each distributor at a successful level requiring a large number of people underneath them, I realized it would take the population of eight planet Earths for that statement to approach the realm of truth.

In our current business, Heart of Business, I'm very clear that our approach is not for everyone. Some folks will do better with other business development coaches and trainers. We've had clients who haven't thrived with us, and that's normal for any business.

Lying, distorting truth, and leaving out facts sits heavily on our hearts. We often react to it strongly when we ourselves engage in these behaviors. And we have potent reactions, too, when we suspect someone else is leaving something out.

Leaving things out is standard practice for much of the marketing industry. For example, I discovered that in the United States, even when a bottle of olive oil only has "olive oil" listed in the ingredients and nothing else, it still might not be 100-percent olive oil. Other kinds of oils can be mixed in.

This kind of rampant lying is enraging. How do we move in a world where we are pelted by so many untruths? Many of us have become numb to it, and only occasionally enraged.

One of our core teachings at Heart of Business—and something I find myself repeating to clients often—is this: "Almost all marketing and sales problems can be solved with honesty."

If you didn't know you can be both honest and effective, *of course* you would avoid marketing.

Let's talk about another way marketing is done terribly: namely, using pain points to retraumatize people. Mentioning problems, challenges, and struggles is a fairly standard practice in marketing. But big problems arise when these issues are then amplified intentionally so that a sense of deep internal agitation is created in the potential buyer. For many people, this agitation can be very intense, because the advertising scheme touches on a very real, distressing, and abiding issue in their personal lives. They thus experience retraumatization—often unawares.

Naturally, people want to stop the pain. In this kind of unethical marketing, once someone is agitated, marketers offer a way out. Relief comes by way of purchasing the product or service.

Intentional agitation of the would-be consumer happens a lot in my own industry, business development. People have intensely personal hopes and dreams wrapped up in developing a business. They also have survival fears. They worry about not being able to make rent and buy food. All this becomes a ball of agitation.

That sense of worry, of intense unease, is then used to sell unethically priced business-development programs and services. At Heart of Business, we've had so many clients come to us after they've maxed out their credit cards and spent thousands, even tens of thousands, on business development that got them nowhere. It tears at my heart.

Now, I believe it's important to mention people's challenges and struggles in your marketing. But you can do this without traumatizing your audience. If you can see each person as whole, unbroken, and beautiful, and if you witness any challenge they are facing with genuine empathy, then they can feel seen. If they feel seen, and you make the effort to say that your offer is not the only way to get help, then it can be much more ethically aligned. In fact, insisting on an empathic approach that humanizes people is the difference between manipulation and compassion in marketing. And, to my mind, it is key to business ethics.

A third way marketing is done badly is by creating pressure to act quickly. Fake deadlines, fast-action discounts, and artificial scarcity all create a sense of urgency which affects the buyer's ability to make choices.

Not long ago, my wife and I were in conversation with a company that was trying to sell us an upgrade to our gutters. The salesperson told us that if we made the decision to purchase right then and there, without thinking it over, they could take two thousand dollars off the price.

Because I knew this was an unethical tactic, we immediately said no. In fact, I paused to tell the salesperson, "You know, I actually train people in heart-centered selling, and your tactic is unethical." My wife and I later found someone to clean out our gutters for a fraction of the price. We did not need new gutters.

We encountered the same tactic from a company who installs solar panels. They offered us a twelve-thousand-dollar discount if we decided immediately. We declined and found out soon afterward they had quoted us a price that was half again as much as what competitors were charging.

If you didn't know that the pressure approach is a commonly used unethical sales tactic, it would be hard to resist such a big "discount." Even really savvy people get caught by this method.

Honest businesses charge honest prices. Discounts are sometimes offered in good faith, but never in a way that tries to circumvent the consideration process.

At Heart of Business, we offer early-bird discounts for folks who sign up for our courses before the final deadline. However, our audience has days, sometimes weeks, to consider the deadline. And we're always up front to say the discount is offered to avoid everyone signing up at the very last minute, thereby overwhelming our administrative staff trying to get everyone set up in time. If someone comes across our early-bird deadlines at the last minute, we always give them a day-or-two grace period to take advantage of it.

That's the difference between ethical use of legitimate discounts and deadlines versus unethical use that tries to short-circuit the customer's decision-making process.

When business is done well, people are neither manipulated nor harmed. The task of challenging slimy sales tactics requires educating and empowering not only business owners, but consumers as well. I care deeply about this, which is why I wrote a whole guide about unethical sales tactics. The guide talks about ethical pricing in business development, as well. It's free, and you might like it. It's called *Don't Buy Now!*

www.heartcenteredbusinessbook.com/resources/dont-buy-now

Thus, sadly, most people's experience of marketing is profoundly linked to experiences of lying and psychological manipulation. We all know how awful that feels on the buying side of things. As a business owner, it makes perfect sense that you'd resist participating in it! *Of course* you don't want to be involved with marketing, if that's what marketing really is.

Let's pause to notice and give space to your responses of grief, anger, and even rage. Marketing has been used to harm so many people. Even with (or perhaps because of!) my spiritual practice, so much terribleness in marketing sometimes makes me want to throw things.

Your resistance to marketing is a sign of integrity. It points to a strong, caring heart. It is not something to be overcome or a weakness to be healed. Your heart has wisdom in it.

After the grief and rage, this is one of those places where we get to practice our capacity to be with uncomfortable emotions. We lean into something that looks terrible and see if we can find the love. And you can find the love in marketing—because it's there.

I assure you, there is a radically different way to approach it: one that doesn't sacrifice effectiveness yet enables you to stay firmly rooted in honesty and care. To find it, you must let go of the idea that marketing is about attracting people.

It's Not about Attraction

Attraction has to do with how folks are pulled in a certain direction. You could call it gravity. Or, perhaps more honestly, you could call it love. Attraction exists within the province of love. Trying to manufacture attraction feels as gross as trying to manufacture love. It ends up feeling dishonest and slimy.

Attraction feels clean when love is present. It's the natural pull you feel when you know there is care involved, when your heart knows something that maybe you can't perceive consciously.

The challenge is that we've all been hurt before when love is present. Someone can have sincere love in their heart and still act in harmful ways because of habits or reactions we've learned earlier in life. The heart feels the pull, and the self says, "Am I going to get my heart broken? Am I going to be hurt?"

I want to suggest that it's not marketing's role to attract people, to pull people in. Instead, marketing's job is to offer safety to those who are naturally attracted by the love and care present in your business and your own heart.

What if marketing didn't mean you're trying to convince anyone of anything? What if you could just let go of trying to "attract" people? What if you could release the tension of needing to convince people that you are relevant?

What if, instead of that mess, marketing meant cultivating a sense of safety and trust with those who are naturally pulled toward you and the good things you provide through your business? Imagine marketing as simply a matter of filling your heart with love, seeing people who need your help, offering care and support, and allowing those who are drawn to come.

Allow yourself to slow down, to take a full breath. And maybe a sigh of relief.

Wait ... but does that really work?

You bet it does! In fact, it works especially well on the more personal, human scale on which small businesses operate.

True Marketing Communicates Safety

Marketing's true role is to convey safety to people. What does this mean?

Remember from chapter 1 that quote in Islam attributed to the Divine: "I was a hidden treasure and I yearned to be known, so I created the creation in order to be known." According to this teaching, a yearning to be known is at the heart of creation, and the spark of yearning to be known lives in each of us. Being known, being witnessed, is nourishing to each of us.

Safety is created when someone feels truly seen as whole, despite challenges. In other words, when I am witnessed as I am, without judgment, I feel safe.

Something I've learned along the way is that when we're physically in front of someone, they can feel seen by the nameless presence in our eyes. There is a way of communicating through the eyes that makes people feel truly seen and received.

When we're not physically with someone—for instance, when they read our website, or another communication—being seen happens as we empathetically name someone's identity, values, and/or situation.

Contrast this approach with dysfunctional marketing, wherein the pain someone might be experiencing is named, highlighted, and amplified through repetition to bring about agitation in the reader or viewer. Knowing this agitated state is extremely uncomfortable, the manipulative marketer then offers their solution as the way to banish the discomfort: "If you're experiencing chronic back pain, you may be wondering if your formerly active life is now doomed! You worry you'll never be able to lift your child again. Luckily, our patented, only-available-from-us-solution, for a limited time only, means that your child won't grow up without your hugs."

Ugh. I felt sick just writing that.

In heart-based marketing, we can name the challenge someone is going through with empathy, in a way that allows the reader to slow down and take a breath. That slowing down allows them to feel a bit safer. It also allows them to evaluate whether an offer is something for them (or not) while they're in a less reactive state.

It's the difference between the manipulative example above and something like this: "There are a lot of folks who have chronic back pain. Life is livable, for sure, but it's not easy, and there are cherished activities that are hard or impossible to get to. You really know that healing is possible. It's just been hard to make the kind of progress that you've seen other people make, even though you've tried several things. There's no one right answer for everyone. Yet we've had good luck with many people when it comes to helping them heal chronic back pain. We invite you to look, to see if what we do might work for you."

With this approach it's still important to name the problem. Due to all the terrible experiences they've had with marketers using pain points in unethical ways, many heart-centered business owners only want to talk about the positive.

But if you only mention the positive, then struggling people won't see you as relevant. The truth is that the pain and struggle are real in their lives. To ignore that is to fail to see them. It's important to meet people where they are. People who are struggling benefit greatly when they are witnessed in their struggle without judgment. It's a large part of what helps them feel safe. If you only talk about possibility, most people will react, "Oh, that's nice for other people. I could never do that, because of my struggle with [x]." Or, "Oh, that sounds nice. I'll get to that after I solve this problem I'm facing."

The underlying attitudes and assumptions you hold toward people matter profoundly when it comes to communicating safety. It's crucial, for example, to respect others' sovereignty: that is, to hold in your heart the belief that all your potential clients are adults, with hearts, minds, and the ability to make choices for themselves.

When you never presume you know better than another person about what's right for them, you remove any inclination to somehow convince them to decide one way or another. Immediately, you are freed from the burden of most unethical marketing strategies. More importantly, your inward assumption communicates to people that they are seen, respected, and honored. This helps them feel safe.

The Hardest Part of Ethical Marketing

Some aspects of ethical marketing require more intentionality and effort than others. Learning how to communicate clearly, in language and concepts that your audience can actually understand is one such aspect.

There is a natural gap between expert/practitioner language and the language your clients use. Your task is to bridge that gap.

Let's revisit the example of an acupuncturist. They might assess a patient and say, "The energy is blocked, and wind (one of the elements in Chinese medicine) is out of balance." But what the patient is saying is, "I feel like complete crap." To communicate ethically and effectively, the acupuncturist needs to create a bridge through language. One example might be, "I bet you've been feeling exhausted! Let's work on freeing up more of your body's natural energy and flow so you can get back to the things you used to do."

If you want your potential audience to feel safe, it's essential to stop communicating with them as if they are, or want to become, practitioners of your modality. The secret is that they don't care about your modality. Not really.

It's hard to hear. I'm absolutely in love with Sufi healing, and I've read so many business books because it's interesting to me. Our clients don't want any of that, not really. They just want their businesses to work.

Imagine someone approaches your business and doesn't feel seen; they don't feel like you acknowledge their struggle. Then you try to teach them about what you do as if they are going to study and practice it themselves. I promise you they won't feel safe, you won't feel relevant to them, and they'll leave.

It can be a hard shift to make: seeing the world from your client's perspective and learning to use language that they use. It can feel like betraying or watering down your work. It can feel as if you are "dumbing down." It can also feel surprising, as in, "Why isn't everyone as fascinated about this as I am?"

It's not that you can't, or shouldn't, discuss important ideas. Obviously, this book is full of Sufi teachings, so I didn't shy away from sharing the depth of my own approach. But I understand that you probably aren't interested in becoming a Sufi healing practitioner. I have worked hard to recognize this and accept that you don't need to geek out with me on all the intricacies of this thing I love so much. I share what I share because I feel it's useful to *you* in the context of developing your business.

The effort you need to make in your marketing is this exact shift. It's learning, experimenting, and trying different types of communication until you find what resonates with your audience. This is not about coercion. It's about helping people feel seen and heard, so that the relevance of your work to their struggles becomes obvious.

The task of finding language that connects with people is closely linked to another crucial task: namely, finding your niche or "target market." Without having clarity about who you are trying to reach, there is no way to have a conversation with them in which they feel seen and cared for.

Whom Are You Helping?

At Heart of Business, we had a client who taught conflict resolution. The principles and approaches she offered would work equally well in any number of situations. So on her website, this client attempted to show how her principles applied to many contexts, whether family conflict, corporate, or otherwise.

As we worked with her, she came to see how impossible it was for her website to really speak both to parents struggling with conflict in their families *and* to corporate leaders struggling with conflict on their teams. While it's conceivable that any of her website visitors could be both parent and corporate team leader, the details, the intimacy, and the context of the two situations are vastly different. In her effort to help everyone, she ended up helping very few. However, once she chose one of these audiences (and oriented her website content solely in that direction), her business gained clarity and momentum.

Remember, a business is defined not by what you *do*, but by whom you help and what you help them with, which is that first element in the First Stage of business development discussed in chapter 4. It is not an acupuncture practice; it's a practice that helps people with chronic illness (if that's the focus). It's not a business-coaching practice, it's a practice that helps small business owners who want to make a difference in the world and need to make a profit (that's us, here at Heart of Business.)

The true purpose of marketing is safety, and safety arises out of being seen. And people feel seen when their details and identity are seen. That's why niching is so important not only to do business effectively, but also to do it in a way that feels great. If your business is defined by what *you do*, then you are looking at yourself. However, if your business is defined by *whom you help and what you help them with*, then your business is focused on seeing your audience and helping them, which really feeds the deep human desire to be of service.

Not incidentally, centering your business on those whom you help means you can add skills without fundamentally changing your business. I've had clients come to us who've said, "I have three businesses! A deep-tissue massage business, an aromatherapy business, and a Reiki healing business."

I assured them that they didn't have three businesses. Instead, they had one business, focused on one type of client (or a few related types of clients). And they had a whole bag of skills they brought to help each client. This approach eliminated making a client choose whether they were getting massage, aromatherapy, or Reiki. It also eliminated the problem of charging different amounts for different kinds of sessions.

Great marketing exists at the heart of the business; it's not a veneer that gets put on top. It's something that helps you focus on being of service to people who need your help.

If you embrace this understanding of marketing, your heart can rest much more easily.

I want to invite you to muse about this question: To whom might I be of service? Too many business development programs treat this question way too lightly. Even business coaches can fall prey to focusing too much on themselves and not enough on their clients.

Truth is, business owners tend to struggle with identifying the folks they serve. But it's a worthy struggle. Let me make it a bit easier by mentioning a few things before you dive in.

First, whom you serve in your business is not a Divine calling. From a Sufi perspective, your Divine calling is to express the qualities of your heart in the world, and to find the love in every little thing. Whether you are a tinkerer, a tailor, or a candlestick maker, as the old nursery rhyme puts it, doesn't matter.

So, rather than making the decision about whom to focus on for your business a Divine quest of some sort, know that you can simply pick a group that makes you happy—people you really enjoy helping—and rest there.

A second thing I want to mention is that it's not a marriage. You can pick an audience to focus on for your business, then change it later. I sometimes advise people to pick a focus and make a commitment to it for six or twelve or eighteen months, just to see what it's like and whether they can get some traction. Although sometimes people do want or need to pivot away from their initial choice, often they don't. And even if they do, having gained traction in one focus, they are often much faster coming up to speed with any pivot they do make.

Third, please be compassionate with yourself. It is unlikely that you will land on the perfect niche just by doing the exercise I include below. Hold this lightly, play with it, come to it with an open heart. It's not unusual for someone to work on this for four, eight, or twelve weeks. When it starts to get longer, that's when I advise them to just pick something and see if they can get some traction, rather than getting caught in perfectionism.

Let me invite you into a short exercise that can help you begin to play with the question of audience.

Who is your business here to help?

1. Read through these illusions:

"I must take care of everyone who shows up."

"I must make sure that everyone gets all their needs met."

"It's my job to help everybody, no matter what."

"I'm not allowed to follow my heart."

Stop. Just stop. Read through those illusions again, slowly. Do any of them have a grip on you? Or perhaps another one that's similar? Name the illusion that you are believing.

Example: Ouch, it hurts to read these. "I must make sure that everyone gets all their needs met" zings me to the core. And another one not on the list: "If everyone doesn't approve of me, I'd better not do anything."

2. This is a good time to begin the Remembrance or other heart-connecting practice of Remembering Oneness and Love. From your love of truth, with the support of your heart's connection, say no to the illusion, then turn your back on it. What do you notice when you do that?

Example: After reading the illusions, it was hard to come back into my heart. I took a few minutes to settle back down, but eventually my breath deepened and I became aware of

*a warmth in my chest. I realized I didn't need to say "no!"
out of anger or fight. Instead, I could just calmly say, "No,
this isn't right," and turn my back on it. What a relief ... my
heart feels flooded with peace and ease.*

3. **Ask your heart: who is your business really here to
   help? Who are you most nourished by in helping?**
   Take your time. Don't rush. Give yourself some gentle
   spaciousness here. As you get any little bits of clarity,
   write them down. Breathe. Relax. Open.

   Note: This is not your One Compelling Sentence, or
   even marketing language of any sort. This is just for
   you. You may not even get tremendously clear. You are,
   however, opening the path to clarity. So ask, trust your
   heart, and see what comes. Say yes to whatever comes.

   *Example: As I began this, I could feel little nibbles of the
   "should" still hanging around, and as I said "no" again,
   I realized my heart was asking, "Is it really okay to enjoy
   myself? To do what I love?" And I heard "yes." I realize
   there are some clients I really like and some I don't. I realize
   I really enjoy the issues that older women bring more than
   almost anything else. I realize that's what feeds my heart.
   What a relief to just say that.*

Keep breathing. It's going to be okay. In fact, it's going
to be more than okay. It's going to be wonderful. Because
when you allow yourself to focus on the people you most
like to work with, those people will be able to find you
much more easily.

Understanding why there's so much pain around marketing means there's nothing wrong with you for having reactions. And learning the true purpose of marketing and how your heart can be aligned will hopefully bring you some compassion, relief, and a clear path forward. Which is good, because in the next chapter, I want to get more detailed about what you need to be effective with marketing, in the Three Journeys of Marketing.

✧

Things to Remember:
- Your reactions to marketing are justifiable. There is a long history of unethical marketing with profoundly negative consequences. That is worthwhile to be cautious of.
- It is possible to do marketing ethically, with love and care, if you're willing to lean in.
- The true purpose of marketing is not attracting people to you, but rather communicating safety to those who are naturally attracted to the care and service you provide.
- Problems and challenges are important to communicate in your marketing—not to create reactions, but to give empathy and help your potential clients feel seen, cared for, and safe.
- The underlying assumption in all marketing is that your potential clients are whole, sovereign beings; they are not broken in any way.
- Niching—knowing whom you can help and what you can help them with—is at the heart of what your business is, and is also the foundation of what makes business so fulfilling.

CHAPTER 7

The Three Journeys of Marketing

Sonia was struggling with her marketing. She was sure it was broken and needed to be fixed.

She had enough trust in me to invite me in to take a look and offer my thoughts, even though that's a terribly vulnerable thing to do. When I looked, I saw that her marketing wasn't broken at all. She was publishing articles, and people were responding. But new people weren't showing up, and she also wasn't seeing folks sign up for her offers.

It's not that what she was doing wasn't working. But there were elements missing that needed to be filled in.

I've worked with thousands of people over the last twenty years. This experience has taught me that marketing is perhaps the trickiest issue for small business owners, and it's what I find myself helping clients with the most. Yet where many folks think their marketing is broken, it's sometimes working really well. As in Sonia's case, their marketing isn't faulty, it's just incomplete.

Here's a helpful image: think of a bridge with a section on either shore and a middle section where people cross. The first part of the bridge, on the closer shore, can be working fantastically. People can begin to cross over. But if either of the other sections are unfinished or absent altogether, people can't make the journey to the other side.

That's what I mean by incomplete. When business owners think their marketing is broken, it's often the case that they've been working hard on one aspect of marketing, but they don't know there are other crucial marketing elements needed in order for people to arrive in their business.

I want to introduce you to the Three Journeys of Marketing. My hope is that this will invite you into a much more open-hearted, easy relationship with your marketing. As I covered in the previous chapter, marketing has a terrible modern history. In view of that, it's important to my own heart that you find the space within you to hold two truths simultaneously.

The first truth is that your feelings about marketing are legitimate and have wisdom in them. They are not reactions that you have to "get over." They are guideposts to helping you chart a healthier relationship with this necessary aspect of your business.

That "necessary" bit is the second truth: your business must be visible to other people, especially to new people. We call that "marketing," which simply means being visible in the marketplace. Historically, this meant literally showing up in the public square with the other farmers and craftspeople. To market was to participate, to offer, to just be visible in the human community. And this, at heart, is what marketing still means—even though, in our culture, the modalities and scope are usually far different.

My hope is that the previous chapter on the True Purpose of Marketing, and now this chapter on the Three Journeys of Marketing, will help you see that marketing can be very different from the unethical, harmful marketing strategies you've witnessed. I hope you, like many of our previous clients, don't have to break your heart or hurt other people to make your business visible.

Many Heart of Business clients have surprised themselves by coming to like or even love marketing, precisely because it can be something very different from what they've experienced elsewhere.

What Unethical, Ineffective Marketing Gets Wrong

Years ago, when I was a faculty member with my spiritual lineage's Sufi Teacher Internship Program, I was giving a presentation on marketing to the student teachers. One of my main points was that people need time to prepare before they make a significant purchasing decision (like joining a Sufi school or beginning to work with a spiritual healer).

The pushback came immediately. "I can see where that's true for many things, but this is spiritual work. People feel it in their heart and jump in a moment." Even my co-faculty for the class questioned me on this point.

"I'm open," I told them. "Let me ask some questions, and you can tell me what's true for you." As I went around the room and questioned each person, every one of them, without exception, admitted that they hadn't jumped in a single moment.

Even those who had met the main spiritual teacher and decided immediately on meeting him described a previous journey spanning anywhere from six months to ten years. In that time, they had met other spiritual teachers, read books, and taken workshops. Each person had a lot of preparation before deciding to study with this particular Sufi lineage.

I'm explaining all this because there is an assumption among most newer small business owners that there is some magic phrase—some perfect way of saying what you do—that will take a complete stranger and turn them into a client instantly.

It's just not true. That phrase doesn't exist.

Now, there's good reason for believing this myth. When you're new in business, your initial clients are often the kind of people who've had a journey of preparation. They're ready to work with you because they've had contact with other people, similar offers, and contexts akin to yours. Maybe they've been considering working with someone like you for months or even years. So when they meet you, they jump right in.

However, in any mature business, it's only a very tiny percentage of clients who say "yes!" as soon as they meet you, based purely on intuition and preparation. Most, instead, take time after they meet you. They wait to sign up until the timing is just right.

Unethical and/or ineffective marketing (which covers a lot of marketing in general) doesn't take this waiting and consideration period into account. Many marketing strategies I've seen say, effectively, "Buy from me right now—or there's the door. Jump in immediately—or forget about it." It's basically a high-pressure ultimatum.

The length of time it takes someone to make a significant purchasing decision is one of the most underestimated dynamics in business. The potential client looks at your offer and considers it. But it might take a while before they're ready to buy, and this may be due to any number of legitimate reasons. Maybe the timing is off in their life. Maybe the resources don't line up. Maybe they're just not ready.

Unethical marketing would call this a "lack of commitment." No. It doesn't signal a lack of commitment. It says they are honoring *all* the priorities in their life and considering carefully to determine when they are ready.

This arises directly from something I mentioned in the previous chapter. It's far more ethical and heart-centered to operate from the assumption—the truth—that your potential client is a sovereign adult, the best person to make choices in their own life. This includes whether they want to hire you or not, and if they do want to hire you, what their own sense of right timing is.

I get emails all the time from people who tell me, "I've been on your email list forever," or "I've been following you on social media for months or years, and I'm now ready to step in." Without effective marketing, especially something structured, folks like that will disappear before they ever reach out to you.

It feels good to my heart that we can honor people's timing. At Heart of Business, no one needs to feel rushed or pressured to jump in before they're ready. This is one of the biggest reasons I want you to know the Three Journeys of Marketing. The journeys I discuss below respect the autonomy and freedom of potential clients. Marketing that's grounded in such respect is not only more ethical than the buy-or-leave approach; it's also more effective.

Introducing The Three Journeys of Marketing

Let me relieve your curiosity and just briefly name the Three Journeys. Then we'll go more deeply into each one.

4. **The First Journey of Marketing: Becoming Known**

5. **The Second Journey of Marketing: Nourishing Those Waiting**

6. **The Third Journey of Marketing: Supporting Referrals**

These three journeys are a repeating cycle that help your business fly. New people find out about you but aren't pushed to buy too quickly and naturally move into a Second Journey relationship. Your consistent connection through a Second Journey strategy helps the right people purchase within timing that makes sense to them. A robust, systematic Third Journey means your clients and others in your network help make your business visible to others, who enter at the First Journey and the cycle begins again with these new people.

Understanding these journeys helps your marketing be much more relaxed and in alignment with marketing's true purpose: the creation of safety. It should be understood that any particular marketing strategy might apply to more than one journey at a time. And that's okay. After all, business, like life, isn't neat and tidy.

The First Journey: Becoming Known

When most people think "marketing," once they get past their initial negative associations, they think mainly of tactics that belong only in the First Journey of marketing. This is the marketing focused on making connections with brand new people—folks who don't know you and don't know your business. The intention of First Journey Marketing is not to make the sale.

Let me repeat that. When you take on what I call First Journey Marketing tasks, the intention is not to make the sale. The goal, rather, is to create safety for someone to come closer. When they come closer to your business, they can then tell whether it's relevant to them and whether they sense the attraction in their heart.

If someone doesn't buy right away, you haven't failed. You're only on your first leg of the journey, after all. What a relief!

Marketing is a journey, a relationship, not a smash and grab for clients. Failure to understand this is where a lot of the marketing "yuck" comes from. Activities like giving talks, doing webinars and social media, advertising, and networking with new people are all First Journey activities. For the most part, they are intended to make contact with new people and welcome them into a safe and supportive relationship with your business.

If you're trying to get new people to buy immediately in a webinar or talk, or while networking, you can see how that quickly becomes pressure-filled and somewhat repulsive. If a business owner thinks immediate sales are supposed to happen in the context of a free webinar, then of course they resort to high pressure, manipulative sales tactics to get the sales. Why? Because, quite naturally, most people won't buy on the first contact without manipulation.

What if there was no pressure to make an immediate sale? What if your heart's intent was not to secure a paying customer straightaway, but instead to make contact and allow them to decide if they want to step forward into the Second Journey?

For about a year, we at Heart of Business tried our hand at social media webinar sales. They didn't work the way we had imagined they would because we refused to use the typical high-pressure sales tactics. The webinars did, however, help bring new people to our newsletter. Then, over the next six to twelve months, we had plenty of people purchase from us. This is a great example of the Three Journeys of Marketing in action. It's always a little slower, more organic, more natural, just as most healthy relationships grow. But it's still robustly effective.

Here are just a few examples of First Journey Marketing strategies you might try:

- Offer a free webinar without a strong sales pitch.
- Create content, like an article or video, and share it on social media so it ends up in front of new people.

- Engage in social media advertising, or advertising of any kind, but without directly selling an offer. Just make an invitation for people to join your audience.
- Attend networking events where you meet new people.

Some of these tactics have some overlap with Second or Third Journey Marketing. There is rarely a sharp line dividing them. What distinguishes the journeys from one another is the intention behind them. With the First Journey, the intention is all about creating opportunities for new people get to know you. Then, from there, you can invite people to take the next step with you and join your Second Journey Marketing.

While engaging in First Journey tasks, I encourage you to be explicit about your no-pressure approach. Speak to people directly about it. For instance, in a webinar or other talk, you might say something like: "If you already know us and trust us, you may be interested in our upcoming course. If you're new to us and still learning whether this approach resonates, don't feel pressured. Stay on our newsletter list, check out our content, see if our approach works for you." Granting people space and time is not only effective in getting new clients; it also feels good to the heart, because it honors people's autonomy.

Now, there will be that small percentage of brand-new people who are ready to jump in with you immediately. You don't have to worry about them; they're going to step forward anyway and make themselves known. Rather than putting a lot of effort into selling to the few who would have stepped forward anyway, you can just let them do that on their own. Instead, focus on bringing care to the folks who need more time to build trust with you.

Which, of course, is the job of the Second Journey of Marketing.

The Second Journey: Nourishing Those Waiting

The intention of the Second Journey is to allow someone to build trust with you over time—whatever time they need. This could be a day, a week, a month, or years.

A business remains full of paying clients and customers when there's enough people in the Second Journey that, at any one time, there are plenty to step into your offer(s), without you having to push anyone.

It's often said that to be in sales, you must remain unattached to the outcome of whether any particular person buys or not. It's a profound and challenging spiritual practice to remain unattached when you're talking to one of two potential clients in an entire month and your business is struggling. It's much easier (and doesn't require the spiritual alignment of a saint) to maintain non-attachment when you have a larger audience: an audience with enough people ready to say yes even when plenty of others say no or "not right now."

It bears repeating: the defining intent of Second Journey Marketing is to build trust over time. To do this, you need to provide regular, consistent content that will nourish people and invite them to take the next step.

That content can take many different forms. Examples include videos, free courses, talks, blogs, webinars, social media posts, newsletters, free workshops, articles, and window displays at retail locations. The creativity comes less in the *what*, and more in the *how*. For instance, will your content be short and inspirational? Long and nuanced? Comedic? Serious?

Rachael K. Albers of RKA Ink, someone I respect highly, has leaned into her acting experience and created videos acting out exaggerated caricatures of bad or unethical marketers to make her points. They are hilarious—and so true. Another friend and colleague, Eric Klein of Wisdom Heart, uses art to create drawings he calls "Dharma Doodles" that make spiritual concepts easy to understand at a glance. He also uses guitar-playing to help create meditations.

It's easy, of course, to compare oneself to those who have a unique talent, like acting or art, and feel like you come up short. But truthfully, I've seen many people without any standout artistic skills still bring humanity, love, and creativity to their communications. They've moved and nourished their audience in ways that reflect who they are and what they bring.

If what you offer is relatively consistent, from your heart, and speaks to your audience's needs and interests, you will succeed with your Second Journey Marketing.

People sometimes ask whether it's worth it to publish content regularly, especially when they may not always hear back from their audience. I regularly publish e-newsletters, and sometimes I hear nothing back from anyone, despite having an audience of thousands.

Nevertheless, sometimes I do hear back. After a newsletter goes out, a stream of replies like this one may come: "Thank you for your words, Mark. I always get great comfort from them and I continue to successfully run my business through the ups and downs of life because of what I have learned from you and your courses. Thank you."

We extend Second Journey content not to get likes or feedback (although that always helps). Rather, the point of our offerings is to deliver our help and our presence to people. In effect, our communications say, over and over: "I'm here. I care. We're in this together." Your content is a chance to give wholeheartedly, unreservedly, generously—and yet in a way that is sustainable for you.

Some find that putting out regular content can feel grueling, exhausting. It doesn't have to be that way. Yes, it is work. But there are ways to make it lighter. For one, you can learn how to create content more easily, such as we teach our clients. You also can pick a more sustainable schedule. We publish weekly, but there are many who only send out content twice or even once per month.

Finally, you can make different kinds of content. Maybe you publish one longer article or video, but the second one just focuses on one small part of that article. Or you make the second one an inspirational quote or something else relatively light and easy to create.

Not every business has to have a heavy publishing schedule, but, for the reasons we're discussing here, it's my opinion that most businesses can benefit from at least some content.

This heart-centered, no-pressure method allows folks to get to know you in a way that gives them distance. The gift of time and space means people can approach in a way that feels really honoring to them.

Imagine a bright, welcoming cafe that sits on a street corner. The servers smile and say "hi" to passersby. Periodically, a small table with a plate of free brownie samples is placed by the front door. A dog water dish sits on the ground, as well. Inspiring quotes line the pristine, clear windows. Somebody walks by once and stops to taste a brownie. The next time they walk past, they stop to let their dog drink some water. The third time they pause to read what's written in the window. The fourth time, they go in and order something.

By providing your ongoing, nourishing presence, you allow people to find out that you are real, you're going to be there, and you're going to keep showing up. And it allows them to decide within their own timing when they're ready.

Let me repeat a point about email newsletters: yes, there's room for you amid the untold number of e-newsletters already out there. The truth is, there are people who really need to hear your voice. Your presence is important, and people want to connect with you. Email newsletters can still facilitate that connection.

Here's a creative example of a combination of First Journey and Second Journey Marketing—one that may inspire and encourage you if you fear your written content will generate only cricket chirps.

A bike mechanic once lived near us. I rode my bicycle a lot, so I needed a mechanic. I learned about this particular mechanic because he hung flyers around the neighborhood. The flyers communicated much more than: "Hey, bike mechanic here!" Rather, there was a good deal of creativity and interest to them. The guy did drawings, offered storytelling, and even included a bit of humor on these flyers. Every few weeks, a different one went up around the neighborhood.

They caught my attention and spoke to me (First Journey), then I saw them on an ongoing basis (Second Journey). Eventually, I called. Over the years we lived there, I saw his bike mechanic business go from a side hustle in his garage to a full bike shop with employees.

My point? *People still really do read things.* I'm on email lists for local businesses around me. And there's several of them I always read. In fact, I read every single word, because I know the people, and it gives me deeper insight into who they are and how they operate. These e-newsletters deepen my care and trust in the business owners. And yes, I do go and use their businesses.

You don't need a million people on your list. You just need a few hundred, maybe. Larger businesses need maybe a few thousand readers. That's not that many people, and your list can build over time as you clarify your audience and expand your network. If you can stay focused on simply being there—with consistency, authenticity, and helpfulness—then you can embrace the Second Journey of Marketing knowing that your voice *will* reach those who need the help you (and only you) can provide.

The Third Journey: Supporting Referrals

The Third Journey, also called referral marketing, is when your raving-fan clients, colleagues, and other people in your circles and networks refer people into your First and Second Journey Marketing.

The dynamics of referral marketing are often misunderstood, leaving many business owners disappointed at the results. I think this arises because there are a few very visible connection-type entrepreneurs who naturally and effectively make a lot of referrals. You may know one of these folks. They seem to know everyone, and every time you mention something, they know someone who can help or source what you are trying to do. They have an easy way about them; the referral process doesn't feel pushy at all, and it just works.

Because these folks are often so visible in that skill, we miss the fact that most people aren't like that. Most people don't remember to refer. In fact, most people literally don't know *how* to refer.

So by taking on referral marketing consciously in your business and learning the dynamics, you can make it much easier and more effective for people to refer others to you.

But first, a word of caution: be careful using the payment-for-referral approach.

One way many business owners try to increase referrals is through payments. "Refer a friend and get a free session!" You've probably seen people doing it, so think maybe you should do it, too. Please don't jump into this approach.

Author Dan Pink wrote a book called *Drive!* in which he pulled together research about what actually motivates people. Surprisingly, one discovery was that money or other rewards can *de-motivate* people from taking action. One explanation is that it takes a natural impulse of generosity and turns it into a job or otherwise sours the experience. Surprising, I know, but true.

Instead, it's important to know why others (e.g., current or former clients, friends, colleagues) don't refer. Moreover, it's important to understand why, when someone is referred to your business, they don't follow through on that referral and contact you.

One reason is that folks don't know whom to refer. Especially when your work is hard to describe and you don't have a clear audience defined, it's hard for someone to know whom they should send your way. So they don't.

Let's compare two practitioners. First, a chiropractor who specializes in helping active people who have developed back pain return to the activities they love. Second, a spiritual healer or transformational practitioner who helps people access their inner wisdom. I bet you already thought of people who could use that chiropractor. I also bet you're scratching your head trying to think of who to send to the spiritual healer. But if I said that the spiritual healer helps folks who wonder if they need to make a change in their career path and struggle to trust themselves to make big decisions about it, suddenly it's much easier to think of people who might need that help, isn't it?

Another reason people don't refer is deeply related to the first: they don't remember. If I say I have back pain and it's keeping me from gardening, that will trigger an association in your mind, "Oh, I've got this chiropractor who helps people like you." It's instantaneous, what we call the "names and faces" response. Any mention of what the chiropractor does, and names and faces of people who need that help leap to mind without having to think about it.

However, for the original spiritual healer example—without the edit I made—what would someone have to say to trigger an association for that? "My spiritual is broken." It's not something that would come up in the normal course of conversation.

A third reason people don't refer is that they don't know how the referral will be treated. I remember sending a friend to someone I knew who had some kind of herbal healing remedy. That friend came back and told me it was a network-marketing company and the person kept trying to get them to sell the remedy. Ugh; I hadn't realized. It only takes one or two experiences like that to have people be shy about sending folks if they don't know you well.

We've considered some of the reasons the referral process never gets off the ground. Sometimes, though, the process gets started but is never completed. What about people who are referred to you but never follow through by contacting you?

When someone could really use your help but they choose not to reach out, it's usually due to vulnerability. It can feel risky and scary to reach out for help. In order to reach out immediately to a stranger—especially around a personal or spiritual issue—someone either has to be in an extreme situation, or else they really need to trust the person doing the referring.

This happened recently when I had a pretty bad pain in my leg. I asked our neighbors—people we liked but didn't know super well—if they knew someone locally who could help. They came back saying, "Oh yes, this person I love, she always helps me out." I was in enough pain that I called the referral immediately.

But many people won't reach out right away because they aren't in that kind of "must-get-help-now!" situation. How many times have people mentioned service providers to you and you've checked out the website, maybe read their social media or blog, then waited before contacting them for help? That's an absolutely normal response.

At Heart of Business, I emphasize this important point with clients and members of our community: "If you're referring people to us, don't tell them to just call or email. Instead, tell them to go to the website, sign up for the news-letter, check out the content, and make sure that they like our approach first."

Having the Three Journeys of Marketing in place allows someone to check you out from a distance and get to know you and your approach a bit before reaching out. This makes a world of difference.

When asking for referrals, there are some important steps you can take that will help people to arrive at your business. First, be clear about who makes a good referral for you. That is, be precise in describing who is a good client for you, so your referral sources can recognize who to send, like I did with the chiropractor example above. Second, let your folks know what happens when a referral of theirs does contact you. That is, tell them how you follow up. And third, if you have free content, or another way people can check you out from a distance, let your referrers know. This makes it much more likely that a referral may eventually land.

These steps take so much pressure off the referral process and increase the likelihood that it will result in a direct contact or a new paying client.

Over time, you can even develop specialized content to support referrals. One of our clients who did *Feldenkrais*, a type of body work, had made a connection with her city's nonprofit bicycle alliance, which promoted bicycling in the city. They had an annual "bike to work" event to increase biking and decrease car use. She had suggested to them, after building a relationship with someone in their organization, that she could create a video for that event to help people know proper body mechanics for biking. They agreed and shared her video. She was seen by thousands of people in that city.

This is a beautiful example of Third Journey Marketing, where an organization referred people to this practitioner's expert care. But it's more than that, for it also illustrates the First Journey: the referral sent people to her helpful and informative video, a classic example of marketing content designed to engage new people. The video then invited folks to get more information, ushering them into her Second Journey. Here, she had a system in place for maintaining ongoing contact with folks who did sign up. Some of those who signed up liked what they saw and became clients.

Marketing works best when all Three Journeys work together.

If you are consistently finding ways to get in front of new people (First Journey), and consistently educating people who know you and whom and how to refer (Third Journey), and consistently communicating with contacts in ways that build trust over time (Second Journey), then you can see how an audience can grow organically until you have an ongoing flow of clients.

Remember Sonia's story from the beginning of this chapter? She had a clear Second Journey and an inconsistent Third Journey. What was missing was regular, effective First Journey Marketing. When she put that in place—and made her Third Journey a bit more effective—all her efforts began to work together. It also helped for her to learn more about heart-centered sales, so folks felt safe stepping in to hire her. She then could see there was nothing wrong with what she had originally: it was just incomplete on its own.

Marketing is about helping people feel safe, so they can listen to their heart's discernment about whether to buy from you or not. The Three Journeys give people the time and space to make clear decisions for themselves while building trust with you.

Marketing, of course, is not the only thing that makes a business successful. It can be hard to know all the pieces that need to come together, which is what we'll be diving into in the next chapters.

Things to Remember:

- Only a very small minority of people are ready to buy when they first meet you. Most people need time to build trust and find their own right timing to step in.
- Marketing has different aspects to it. By dividing it up into the Three Journeys, you can avoid trying to force people to move too quickly.
- For many business owners, their marketing isn't broken; it's just incomplete, only covering one or two of the Three Journeys.
- Ethical and effective marketing is based on the underlying assumption that you can trust your clients; you don't have to convince them to purchase. They are sovereign adults who are the best ones to be making purchasing decisions for themselves.
- Marketing is, in part, a numbers game. Having a larger audience means that there are plenty of people ready to say yes when others say no. This relieves pressure on any one individual to buy from you because you need revenue.

CHAPTER 8

What Your Heart Needs So Your Business Can Succeed

This chapter and the next are meant to help you get your arms around what it really takes to make your business successful. In this chapter, I discuss the spiritual/heart qualities that I believe to be critical for a successful business owner to cultivate in themself. Then, in the next chapter, I discuss the ten essential nuts-and-bolts elements you need to put in place to really be successful.

All this is meant to create a clear pathway as well as compassion in you—compassion directed both toward yourself and your business. Our imaginations are lightning fast; we want things to take off *now*. But implementation in the world, and in our lives, is much slower.

This chapter will walk you through the inner qualities we encourage you to cultivate on the journey of building your dream.

I'm looking out my office window at the hill where we are planting fruit trees. I can imagine the trees full of fruit in the summer, broad limbs heavy, kids running to pick fruit warm in the summer sun.

In truth, there are currently two small saplings, just planted. Five other holes are pre-dug and filled with compost, waiting for the delivery of five more saplings. Those trees will need care and attention: tasks like co-planting other helpful plants around them and watering in the first year when it's dry. It will be several years before the first fruits are picked from them.

We need compassion to hold the gap between where we are and the vision we can see. Compassion that keeps us from judging ourselves when it takes time to come to fruition. Compassion to understand that nothing is wrong; it's just the pace of nature, the pace of human living, the pace of a sustainable, supportive life.

We also need a reliable map so that we have direction plus a sense of the journey, its length, and what we might encounter along the way. That's in the next chapter. First, let's take a close look at the best inner resources for you to cultivate so you can engage with those nuts and bolts of business in a healthy way.

The Top Five Surprising Heart Qualities

What inward characteristics support the journey from struggling to successful in business? Everyone I know who's walked that road without burnout has learned to embrace these five qualities. Because each business owner is human, their embrace of these qualities was imperfect and inconsistent. Yet these qualities still took root in their hearts. I encourage you to let them take root in yours as well.

The five surprising qualities are these:

1. **Vulnerability**

2. **Creativity**

3. **Trust (or Faith)**

4. **Sovereignty**

5. **Patience**

Each of these qualities has taken on meanings in our culture—sometimes negative—that don't reflect the truth and power of what's available. Let's uncover some surprising things about each of them.

VULNERABILITY

Folks are often surprised when I introduce this quality as central to success. Vulnerability is the ability to say, " I don't know." It's the willingness to risk opening your heart. It's when you say, "I can't do it on my own. Can you help me?"

One meaning of vulnerability is being open to letting things in. Want more money? You need to be vulnerable. Need help from others? Vulnerability again. Learning about your blind spots, or something new about marketing? This too is the province of vulnerability.

On this entire list, I rate vulnerability as the single most important success indicator for small business owners. Without it, you're alone in the world. You can't receive what you need. And it's hard to access the other four qualities without it.

The culture many of us live in often asks us to mask, to protect ourselves, to shut down everything—including true joy and grief. Cultivating vulnerability means going against that. The urgent need for vulnerability asks that we inquire into our fears, to discern between when we are truly unsafe and when we are safe but uncomfortable.

It's worthwhile in this moment to remind you about the teaching on neediness I introduced in chapter 2. This is a vast spiritual topic, but let me restate briefly that neediness itself is healthy. We all have needs, and they are legitimate.

Where neediness sometimes goes astray is when we don't acknowledge it, thus unconsciously bring that neediness to a place where it can't be met. If we have a deep, unfulfilled longing for acceptance, this is best worked out in our heart as a spiritual healing process, potentially with the support of beloved community or a healer. Bringing that deep longing to the sales conversation, or to writing a website—most likely unconsciously—will undermine what you are trying to do.

Think about it: when you're thirsty, you get a drink. When you're cold, you put on a sweater. Yet most of us have been taught consciously and unconsciously to mask our unmet needs around connection, belonging, care, and acceptance, among other things.

Yet these are universal needs, and if they are not tended to, they inevitably come out sideways. Remember that client I mentioned earlier in the book who had significant unmet needs around social connection and community, as many of us do? Their needs were coming out sideways in the sales conversation, leading to two-hour enrollment conversations where she felt like she made new friends but rarely ended up with a client.

Once these needs were acknowledged, *with vulnerability,* she could care for them with friends and community she already had. As a result, her enrollment conversations were less than half as long, and she started to enroll paying clients.

I'll repeat: it's not the neediness itself that is bad. It never is. We just need to attend to it with love and compassion in an appropriate venue or container.

This is even more important to remember because your clients are vulnerable—needy—,and the expectation is that they approach and hire you to help them with that vulnerability. Even if you don't do healing work explicitly, there's still a lot of vulnerability. For the client of an accountant to show up with all their messiness around their relationship with their finances is deeply vulnerable and potentially terrifying.

When you as a business owner are in touch with and actively caring for your own neediness, as well as cultivating your vulnerability in healthy ways, that helps to create a sense of connection, empathy, and safety for your clients and others who need to approach you, themselves vulnerable.

CREATIVITY

There's a deep misunderstanding about creativity. It isn't the power to create something out of nothing, which no human being possesses. Everything a human being does that counts as "creative" involves using something that is already here, then combining it or otherwise changing it into a different form. For this reason, creativity can be understood as the ability to see how unlike things can go together. It's the insight to see what odd or strange things can be combined to be useful, beautiful, or both.

You use your creativity when you generate unique offers. Or find a place to fit your home office when there isn't a spare bedroom. Or spot opportunities and niches.

Creativity is a poetic quality. Successful business owners cultivate this creativity by being willing to question assumptions, to experiment, to be willing to risk failing. Because when creativity succeeds, it can both lift the heart and serve the business.

My colleague Chris Zydel, who has for decades led work she calls "Painting from the Wild Heart," has helped thousands of people discover that even when they have never, ever thought of themselves as artistic or creative, that creativity lives inside them and comes out with a little encouragement.

For me, I love seeing our clients' creativity bloom in the context of their businesses because not only is it impactful in terms of business results, but it also means the business is more fun and feels more like them.

When we speak of the heart, sometimes we mean the profound quality of Divine connection and love. And sometimes we mean the expressions of our personalities, uncensored, that are allowed out to play—that spark joy and connection. Your business can really be 100 percent in alignment with who you are. You can fully express yourself within your business, whether it's the words you use, the offers you create, or how you design your invoices.

Creativity is not just where unlike things meet in joyful expression, it's also where the human personality in all its imperfections and quirkiness meets the Divine: in the heart.

TRUST (OR FAITH)

The stereotypical successful small business owner works seven days a week, late into the night, getting it all done. Ugh. You can't work ten to twelve hours every day and be truly productive—or healthy. Things start to break down. You miss opportunities, fail to perceive miracles. You need spaciousness to run a business.

To get that spaciousness, you need trust. Without the deep trust in your heart that you are going to be okay, you won't be able to leave things on your to-do list—sometimes important things—undone. But you will need to. You absolutely need time to rest, to play, to access your creativity and aliveness.

Trust does not mean what some call unquestioning faith. It does not mean closing your eyes to real concerns or threats. Cultivating trust is very similar to cultivating vulnerability: it is a practice. You must be willing to risk discomfort to see if it works out. And even if it doesn't work out, to find out that you're okay anyway. Trust is learning that the ground beneath you really is solid.

In Sufi terms, trust is considered a Divine quality: we don't create trust, yet we can receive and express it. We can access it. Efforts to force oneself to trust are usually fruitless. They usually mean just acting as if one trusts something when one doesn't—not really. What's more, they often mean there are legitimate concerns that need to be addressed before true trust can be cultivated.

With a new business, of course you're not going to trust it to perform and produce the income you need. You may have noticed that "courage" isn't on the list of five qualities. I consider courage to be a bridge to trust.

Courage is what we need when we don't yet have access to trust. Courage is the willingness to experiment, to try something out, to see if trust can be found there. Trust is a necessary quality to cultivate in yourself so you can truly rest.

Courage doesn't allow you to truly rest because the trust isn't there yet—and it shouldn't be. It's courage you already have. Every time you try something you're not sure will work, you are expressing some amount of courage. There are things you won't have the courage to try because they're a leap too far.

That's healthy. It's okay. Your job isn't to manufacture trust, and it isn't to try to lean too much into courage alone. Your job here is to figure out steps small enough that your courage can be a bridge. As you cultivate trust in the smaller steps, then your bigger steps can rest in that deepening trust.

I don't recommend that clients, for instance, just quit a well-paying job and start a business expecting it to take off quickly so they can keep paying their bills. Instead, courage can allow them to drop things in their life temporarily while they work on the basics of their business, slowly trying things out.

As their business develops, they will come to the point where their courage has enabled them to develop trust in their business to replace their existing income. At that point, they may go to part-time work or quit their job altogether. They may not have complete trust that the new business will absolutely work, but they have enough trust and courage from the smaller steps that they can see how it could work.

That's one way trust is developed and expressed.

SOVEREIGNTY

You are in charge of your business. Of course, it's important to get advice, to learn, to embrace other sources of wisdom and experience to guide you. These are crucial aspects of vulnerability. But when it comes down to it, you set the course.

Your business is a precious being: a vehicle for hopes, dreams, and transformative work in the world. It can provide a living for you and perhaps for others, and it can help many struggling people.

Sovereignty means finding inside yourself the willingness to act—sometimes with less care and more boldness. It means taking actions and making decisions, even if they are at times messy and imperfect. It means being the captain of your ship.

It's important to see that without sovereignty, you don't have a business; you have a job.

Developing sovereignty takes a great deal of humility and vulnerability. Spiritually, we don't own anything, we're not the sovereign. The analogy I use is based on the Arabic word *khalifa*, meaning vice-regent. If you work at a hotel, you are there to be in service to the guests of the hotel. But you don't work for them; you work for the owner of the hotel.

In real life, a hotel owner can be good—or they can be toxic. But the Divine Source, the origin of love from which we are not separate, is what/Whom we work for. Spiritually, you are not the sovereign of your business; you are the khalifa, the vice-regent.

One of our clients had been in the habit of booking their clients all over the calendar, interrupting family time and personal time. When she was able to access her own heart, to access Divine sovereignty as the khalifa of her business, she got a strong message that she did not need to collapse in the face of client requests. She needed to check in with the true Owner, so to speak—her deeper self, as she expressed it.

She developed the habit of not immediately replying to client requests if they were outside her usual work hours. Instead, she said, "Let me check my schedule and get back to you to see if that's available."

Putting that pause in gave her time, sometimes even just a few minutes, to check in with her heart. As my friend Michael Bungay-Stanier, author of *The Coaching Habit*, says, "Sometimes saying no involves saying yes more slowly." That pause gave her access to the Divine quality of sovereignty and enabled a huge, overnight shift in her scheduling.

She was surprised by the strength she felt in her being when she started replying "I'm not available then, how about early next week?" She felt strong, clear, grounded. Equally surprising, she found that most of her clients were fine with it. They took her at face value that she wasn't available. They didn't ask, "Why aren't you available?" because, of course, it was none of their business. Whether it was another client, a family dinner, or even just wanting to take a nap, she's not available.

The Sufis teach that the heart naturally wants to be in service. We go astray when we put ourselves deeply in service to the ego of a human being. This is how tyranny happens. However, when we put our hearts in service to the Source of Love, that gives us a powerful support— because we're not just saying no and standing up for ourselves. We're saying no because we're saying yes to love. Being in the position of khalifa gives us a healthy excuse in this context: "I'm just following orders/my heart/my guidance." (Not that you would necessarily say that to a client—although some might.)

PATIENCE

Patience is sometimes misunderstood as a kind of martyrdom: you wait, like a flower on the side of the road, to be picked—or for some magical opportunity to arrive.

That is not *patience* as Sufis understand the quality; that is much more akin to collapse.

Patience is described by Sufi author and scholar Neil Douglas Klotz, in *The Sufi Book of Life*, as a pathway. Klotz teaches that patience is less about passive waiting and more about active resolve. Many times, a relationship or project is a longer-term slow build, and patience feels uncomfortable. But the "heat" of this discomfort is like a "cooking compost pile" which, over time, produces incredible future effects that can't be foreseen.

Patience, in a Sufi spiritual context, is truly more like persistence. It's the dog-with-a-bone unwillingness to not give up on what's true despite hardships, challenges, and longer timelines. Whatever vision you have for your business, you are unlikely to achieve it in a week, a month, even a year. Patience helps sustain you for the journey.

Developing a business is a long-term project. Sometimes you see results that cheer you on. Sometimes you're working on something strategic that may not bear fruit immediately. Allow patience to be developed within you, so you are able to continue despite difficult times. You will necessarily be involved in experiments, in trying things out. For many of the things you do in business, it will be the first time you've done such a thing. It's nearly impossible to be home-run effective the first time you try something—or the second, or even the third. Patience is what will carry you through these attempts. It will allow you to meet disappointments with gentleness, persistence, and strength.

ABOUT MAKING MISTAKES

I want to take a moment to speak about making mistakes. Making mistakes is not really a quality; it's more a willingness in your heart.

Similar to the topic of neediness, the willingness to make mistakes and accept missteps as a healthy and normal part of the journey is so important. It's impossible to do things you've never done before without making some kind of mistake or doing things considerably less effectively than you would with more experience.

Spiritually, this is a large topic in Sufism. My sheikh shared with us, his students, the teaching from the Divine that said if human beings didn't make mistakes, then there would have been an entirely different race of beings created who did.

Mistakes are not just okay; they are holy, sacred. The Sufis believe it is impossible to fully know the Oneness without making mistakes. It would take an entire chapter to fully describe the spiritual implications in this.

Many years ago, when I was teaching a workshop in front of a full room, one of the participants raised their hand and said to me, "I think I get it. The reason you're up there, and I'm sitting down here, is that you were willing to make more mistakes than I've been willing to make."

What I most want your heart to receive is that trying to craft a business, or a life, based on avoiding mistakes is impossible. Not only that, but it makes your life incredibly small and puts business success outside of your reach.

Success only arrives by stepping through, many times, the gate of the mistake. This will mean taking responsibility, admitting when we are wrong, and cleaning things up. And in that process of cleaning up, inviting mercy and gentleness to accompany us. On the path of growth and development, mistakes are many of the stepping stones.

If you truly let this teaching into your heart, then the development of your business—and your entire life—will have so much more ease and joy and love.

Cultivating the Five Qualities

The Five Qualities aren't something you can muster in yourself overnight. You can't create them, buy them, or otherwise force them to show up. They are intangible gifts cultivated through an attitude of intentional receptivity. It's an ongoing practice to deepen your relationship with these qualities. The first step, which you will refine and repeat again and again, is to simply ask your heart to be filled with these qualities.

Four of these qualities are Divine in nature; only vulnerability is truly a human quality. We cannot manufacture the Divine qualities into existence. Rather, we can witness and experience them, as well as receive and express them. And vulnerability is the doorway to receiving the others.

You start by opening yourself to the human quality of vulnerability. Although all the qualities tend to help develop each other, that initial willingness to open your heart and let things in is a necessary first step.

There are many ways to cultivate vulnerability in yourself. Personally, I've found that the most effective method is some kind of spiritual practice because it connects me to a larger reality.

Whether it's devotional prayer, silent meditation, study of sacred texts, music, or yoga or other movement, connecting to Source is a wonderful way to soften your heart without flopping over and collapsing into powerlessness.

In addition to undertaking regular spiritual practice and opening to vulnerability, it helps to identify the quality you're needing in the moment. In other words, rather than trying to get the five qualities all at once, all the time, just notice what you're trying to do. Then see if you can use the vulnerability of "I don't know" to ask your heart which quality is really needed in the moment.

Your heart may surprise you; you may have thought you needed sovereignty to force something through, when in fact you needed patience or trust. Identifying which quality you need allows you to proceed with focus and intention.

Once you've identified which quality you need, you can bring that softness of heart to the quality in question. We tend to have assumptions about what creativity or sovereignty really is. And those assumptions come up most strongly when we need them and wish we had them.

Yet by bringing vulnerability to your approach of patience, for example, you can ask in your heart: "Please help me experience patience in this situation. I'm curious what it looks like here." Again, allow the vulnerability, and be willing to be surprised.

These qualities are intangible and unquantifiable. They can be hard to grasp mentally, especially when you've got a long to-do list and you feel stuck. Yet I suggest you try giving them some attention and space, rather than trying to push through your work on the strategic parts of developing a business. In so doing, you'll find that they begin to take root in your heart and your life. Your business will start to shine with success, too.

What's more, when you cultivate these qualities, it's so much easier to approach the elements you'll want to implement in your business—which we dig into next.

Things to Remember:

- The heart qualities needed are different than what the culture tells us. You can often be successful in business because you don't fit the typical "entrepreneurial" personality stereotypes.
- Vulnerability is the doorway quality, the one that gives your heart access to all the others. Appropriate, healthy vulnerability means you can be nourished for the long term.
- Courage is often only needed for short periods as a bridge to developing trust. You should not be existing solely on courage; it's too depleting.
- It's your business. Don't give your sovereignty over to any other human. Let a strong sense of sovereignty develop within you without losing your vulnerability.
- Patience is not collapse. The persistence of true, Divine patience will see you through.
- Making mistakes is a necessary part of a successful, joyful business.

CHAPTER 9

The Ten Elements of a Thriving Business

Having a healthy business, like having a healthy body, means certain things need to be in place. It takes more than pure love for a business to function. Actually, let me restate that.

It takes bringing love and care to the physical needs of the business for it to thrive. As a paramedic, I learned all about the different anatomical systems of the body and physiologically how they functioned.

I want to do something similar for you with the ten elements of a thriving business, with three intentions.

The first intention is simply that you know what is needed for your business to work. In addition, I want you to have a strong sense of which order to put things in place so that your business can grow most easily.

The second intention is for your heart: that you understand there's a fair amount that goes into developing a business, and that's why you can't develop it in six months. I want you to be prepared for the growth and learning here. It can be a beautiful journey, and you can cultivate compassion for yourself along the way.

The third intention is more profound: I want you to understand the spiritual nature of these ten elements. As I talked about in chapter 3, often folks privilege the internal heart experience as somehow more spiritual and think of the outer structures of the world as less spiritual. That's just not true. Love is found in absolutely everything, and there is nothing that is more or less spiritual than anything else. When you understand the spiritual nature of the physical aspects of your business, it will be easier to find the nourishment in them.

Here's a list of the ten elements:

1. **Business Foundations**

2. **Website and Social Media**

3. **First Journey Marketing (Becoming Known)**

4. **Second Journey Marketing (Nourishing Those Waiting)**

5. **Third Journey Marketing (Supporting Referrals)**

6. **The Garden Path**

7. **Selling**

8. **Money**

9. **Support and Systems**

10. **Celebration and Life Enjoyment**

These elements change and develop through the four stages of business development. For those interested, we have a detailed one-hundred-plus-item checklist in the appendix, and also as a downloadable form to work with, organized by these ten elements and presented according to the stages of business development. In fact, if you're building a business, I highly recommend you go through this list, take some time with it, and really let it sink in—both for self-compassion and to set your compass.

Some of what I'm going to say below I've already introduced in other sections. Here, I'm expanding them and clarifying their context. We've also found with our clients that repetition can be very useful as this map starts to take shape in your mind and being.

Remember that in the process of putting these elements in place, and/or iterating and improving them as your business develops, I highly recommend you be in the practice of cultivating the five qualities from the previous chapter.

1. Businiess Foundations

Everything that exists has things that define the essence of its being, its core identity. Other things may change and often *need* to change over time. But there are certain things at the center of the business that don't change without the core identity of the business changing.

As I've said, I've come to understand that a business is not defined by what it does, by the modality you practice. Rather, it's defined by whom it helps and what problems/challenges it helps those people with. For many people, this is an essential change to the way they understand business.

For example, it's not an accounting business it's a business that helps small business owners track and understand the financial side of their business. Accounting is a skill that is brought to help with that, but it may not be the only skill.

It's not a corporate coaching business; it's a business that helps executives who want their teams to be more independent, creative, and innovative in meeting the company's strategic goals. Coaching is a skill brought to help meet that purpose, but it's not the only one.

I've found that for a business owner to shift or add modalities to what they do is way less radical a change than for a business to change audiences. Changing or adding modalities is like a store adding another product to its shelves: it's not a big deal to the customer. If a massage therapist, Reiki practitioner, or health coach learns hypnotherapy, it's another tool to help the clients they are already working with.

But to change the focus of the business, the audience that it is speaking to, is a radical change in identity. It's like changing from a bike shop to being a florist. Sometimes the change is so radical, you are essentially closing one business and starting over with a new one. For instance, let's say the coach working with executives wanted to stop providing support to corporate executives and instead work with folks on their romantic relationships. This would require such a big change in identity, in language, in focus, that it would really be a brand-new business.

That's why what we sometimes call "niching" is a business foundation. Niching is the way a business creates intimate, trusted connections with people. I spoke about people's resistance to niching in chapter 4. If you're hitting reactions that are stopping you, I recommend you go back and reread that part.

The second part of business foundations when it comes to identifying your audience is writing what I call the Customer-Focused Story (CFS). Your CFS is a story of your business that you use as a template in marketing. The CFS is the Heart of Business term for a five-element message built on what we call "marketing syntax," in non-manipulative, non-exaggerated, non-egoistic language. Briefly, the five elements are: (1) the problem as your client sees and experiences it, (2) what they've already tried to do to fix the problem, (3) why what they've tried to do haven't been as successful as they'd like, (4) what is needed to deal with the problem, and (5) why you're so good at helping people implement what is needed. Each one of these message elements deserves a longer explanation beyond the scope of this section.

Your CFS helps make what you do approachable and understandable. It's a template that can then be used for your website, for sales pages, and for content creation. It's a touchstone and a template for how to communicate with your audience. Our clients have also used it as the outline of a book, and as a way of helping their team and their clients clearly understand what they do and whom they serve.

The CFS is a foundation of the business because it links what you do and whom you serve in a very powerful way. If you change whom you serve, the Customer-Focused Story will need to change, too, in big ways. Otherwise, it's a cornerstone you will rest into again and again.

The third part of business foundations is what in Sufism is sometimes called the "Jewel." Your Jewel is the inner sense of uniqueness, beauty, and power that your heart carries. It is a spiritual element in your heart. It can take years of spending time with your own heart to *deeply* know your Jewel well. However, identifying your Jewel and beginning to embrace it is a big opening for many people.

The Jewel functions more as a catalyst with your clients then as a direct gift. For instance, in a workshop I was helping a client identify her Jewel. She had gone into the exercise thinking that because so many of her clients told her they felt "inspired" after working with her, that her Jewel was "inspiration." But, surrendering into the exercise, she discovered that it was not inspiration. Instead, in her heart she found a deep sense of peace that she longed for herself. She saw that her clients, when they connected with the peace she carried, found a stillness within, and from there they connected with their own inspiration.

The Jewel almost always functions like that. It's a quality that you give to others naturally, without thought, that functions as a catalyst for what happens for your clients when they work with you. Because it's a catalyst, it's not often visible on the surface of your business, and rarely what others can name. Because it's so powerful in its impact, it may be the biggest piece of what attracts people to you.

Surprisingly, it's also the quality you most thirst for yourself. You thrive best when you can receive, witness, experience, and drink in this quality. You give it to others naturally already, yet it can be even more powerful when you become aware of it and consciously stay full yourself. Then the transmission of your Jewel comes from a place of abundance and fullness, like a rain barrel overflowing in a downpour.

I call the Jewel part of your business foundations, but the Sufis would say that this is really your purpose in life. It doesn't mean to do a certain thing or to take on a certain mission. Rather, the purpose is to allow yourself to fill deeply with your Jewel and shine it in the world in everything you do.

I discovered my own Jewel when my sheikh gave me my Sufi name, Abdul'aziz, which means "servant of the Divine Strength." I'd had a difficult, frightened, collapsed relationship with power and strength for much of my life. By embracing and drinking in this Jewel, over many years, I began to carry it more and more in the world. Yet many people don't talk about me as "strong." Instead, they talk about a feeling of safety, kindness, or feeling seen and listened to. In my case, this all arises out of me resting into Divine strength.

It's not necessary to make the Jewel an explicit part of your marketing or messaging; it's an inner journey you are invited to embrace. Often our clients, when working with their Jewels, have a feeling, a sense, a taste of it within themselves for quite a long time before being able to put a name to it. That's perfectly normal.

Together, the niche, the CFS, and the Jewel give your business a solid ground, focus and direction. Without these three, the business can feel all over the place, floppy.

These three set the foundation. They enable your business to show up as a safe haven, as a business that knows itself. A business that clients can recognize and feel safe to step into.

2. Website and Social Media

At this late date I don't think anyone needs to be convinced of the necessity of a website. However, what I want you to understand deeply is that the website is not just for information. Instead, I want you to see that your business's website is a very real way to create and maintain relationships with folks in your audience.

Some businesses have physical locations, like a storefront or a physical office. Other businesses, like ours, operate virtually. I do have an office in my home, but there's no place a client can just show up physically at our business. Either way, your website is important.

The website is one of the first ways that a business starts to operate *without* the owner's presence. When I talk about your business having a heart and a beingness to it that is separate from you, this is one of the ways that spiritual truth manifests physically. Your business's website is out there all the time, connecting with, interacting with, and supporting people even when you're not working.

The content on your website, especially if you're working with a Customer-Focused Story to help create that content, can give empathy to people who are struggling, provide hope for people who feel otherwise stuck, and offer witnessing that allows folks to feel truly seen, which of course is a piece of the healing journey. And your website can have functionality that enables someone to step more deeply into relationship with your work, by allowing them to subscribe to hear from you regularly, sign up for an offer, or reach out with an inquiry.

This beingness is real. The heart-connection is real.

Social media can serve a similar function for the beingness of your business. I know many people have significant, legitimate issues with different social media platforms, and most of those judgments are ones the platforms have earned through acting in bad faith. At the same time, hundreds of millions of people, each one with a heart and with needs, is present within their social media accounts. Your business can show up here and help support relationships with them: real, legitimate relationships of service, care, and vulnerability.

Yes, you will need to put some of your own care and vulnerability into managing your social media, the same way you put it into your website. Yet having a social media presence can allow your business to be in relationship with many more people.

There are sustainable ways to use social media. And there are ways to connect without social media. But, as with many other things, if you feel resistance to social media I ask that you not reject it reactively; instead, lean into what's in your heart around it and see if there's a healthier relationship to be found. You might try using the Your Heart and Money exercise from chapter 2, replacing "money" with "social media" or, more specifically, with one of the platforms you're not wanting to engage with. Then see what your heart discovers.

3. First Journey Marketing (Becoming Known): How your business reaches new people.

We've discussed in-depth the Journeys of Marketing in chapter 7, so I won't reiterate all of them here. What I want to point out is that often some people feel shy being seen in the world, meeting new people, or feeling at capacity in terms of how many relationships they can handle.

If your business is the one handling the First Journey Marketing, if folks are coming into relationship with your business and not you, personally, in your personal social space, this can make a huge difference energetically.

At Heart of Business, our content is often what folks encounter first: for example, articles, videos, and social media postings. Items for which I was present in the creation, but I'm not physically present at the point of contact. And even when I'm leading a webinar in front of new people, which is a type of First Journey Marketing that I do but not everyone has to, it's still the heart of the business that is helping to mediate my relationship with people. I try to be at my best, warm and present, but I'm not being intimate in the way I would with close friends and community.

These relationships occupy a different space, and the business is what holds them. You can rest into a healthy, appropriate veiling and distancing created through First Journey Marketing. This can feel energetically and relationally a lot safer and easier for you to engage with.

You're not out there making friends. You're on a mission, getting help to people who need it. You are being warm and caring, but you aren't inviting these folks who are currently strangers into your close social space.

Let yourself rest into that, and allow the business to be the one mediating your First Journey Marketing.

4. Second Journey Marketing (Nourishing Those Waiting): How your business deepens relationships of trust and care with your current audience.

Second Journey Marketing is an effort that can sometimes feel burdensome to the business owner because it does require ongoing engagement with your audience. This is why it's even more important that your business do some of the lifting here.

So, for instance, when someone joins your Second Journey email list, it's possible to have your business deepen the initial relationship by sending out what is sometimes called a "nurture sequence." This is a sequence of emails that are intended to create connection.

Often, emails like these are misused, when folks employ hard-sell tactics to try to pressure new subscribers into buying quickly. Blah.

Instead, what we do at Heart of Business is send out a sequence of five emails over the course of ten days, each one addressing a different topic. Some are in-depth; some are short and quick. Some are profoundly spiritual; some are much more practical. Some are for those further along the business path; some are for newbies. The stated intention shared with the reader is that we want to provide a variety of content over a short period of time so they can get a real taste of what we do and what we cover, in the hopes that at least a couple of the emails are directly relevant to their situation.

During this time, we do not send regular newsletters or promotional emails. And it's all done automatically.

It's true that creating regular content is work. However, once you've created a certain amount of content, it can be repeated without effort. At one time, I needed to focus on other things for three or four months, so we reached back two to four years, selected a double handful of articles we'd sent out previously, and queued them up to go out again.

Plus, there are innumerable ways to get done the work of producing Second Journey content. I had a client who committed to publishing twice a month to their email list. They focused and got twelve pieces of content done over the course of several weeks. Some video, some written. Some long, some short. Some fun and fanciful, some more in-depth. They queued them up to be published twice per month over six months. They then had five months to do other things before taking another month to create another twelve pieces of content.

Now their business was able to hold the relationships with the audience in a regular way, and the business owner could create the content itself on a schedule that really suited him.

As time moves on, your Second Journey can become more robust. You also build a storehouse of content that can sometimes be reused, continuing to communicate care and have impact far into the future.

5. Third Journey Marketing (Supporting Referrals): How you support your clients, colleagues, and larger network to refer people to you.

When your business is truly contributing to your clients' well-being, it creates tremendous goodwill. They will then naturally want to support you and will be happy tell others about your work.

As I discussed in chapter 4, asking for referrals needs certain kinds of support and information to happen successfully. That information and support can be held by the business in terms of checklists, workflows, reminders, and automated prompts. Those prompts can go directly to your client if appropriate. Or, if the situation feels more delicate, you can create those automatic prompts to come to you so you can make a personal request for referrals in a way that feels good.

Either way, it's the beingness of the business that can hold the Third Journey of Marketing. You don't have to remember through force of will, and you don't have to keep recreating the information and context to ask for referrals each time. Instead, they can be already prepared and made accessible to your clients when needed.

A client who wanted to make sure to ask for referrals twice—once during the initial enrollment of a new client, then with a reminder at session eight in their client package—created this structure. First, she included within the new client packet a brief sheet explaining how much she depends on and appreciates referrals from clients, that of course brand-new clients aren't asked to refer folks before the work has helped them, but that if a client has a good experience with her work, she'll be gently asking for referrals. The sheet then gives a brief description of who makes a good referral, what a new referral can expect, and where a referral can be sent. She then briefly touches on that sheet during the intake process.

Then, within her client notes, there's a reminder in the session-eight spot: "Remind client of referrals." Because it's already been introduced in the beginning, it takes up very little space; she then refers back to the initial sheet and asks the client to send referrals as appropriate.

This structure is, again, held entirely by her business. It's within the client packet, it's within the client notes, it's within her workflow checklist to go over when enrolling new clients. Although she is doing the work, the beingness of the business is holding it, making it less an effort or a product of will power or memory. Thus, asking for and receiving referrals happens much more consistently.

All three of the Journeys of Marketing are important to a thriving business. They create the framework within which to place many things the business can and should hold. This both frees you up to care for your clients and allows you and your business to continually interact with a much larger audience.

6. The Garden Path: Your mix of offers and how they relate to one another.

The work of your business with clients is found within the offers you make. Whether that's individual one-on-one client work, groups, products, done-for-you services (like graphic design or accounting), home-study programs, courses, workshops, retreats, or something else, your paid clients and customers interact with your business through your offers.

Once your business is developed beyond having more than one offer, it's important that the offers have a relationship to one another. Sometimes they are sequenced, meaning first a client does this class, then they do this more in-depth course, then they do this mastery program. Often, they are not sequenced like that. There are good reasons not to in a small business, mainly because you'll have very few potential clients available for later steps in the sequence.

Either way, it's incredibly helpful for your offers to relate to one another, point to one another, and support clients in going from one to another.

This is why we use the term "garden path." There are many types of gardens, from very formal, structured, pristine gardens to more wildcrafted gardens. Yet generally, each garden has a place where you enter the garden space. Also, there generally isn't only one way to move through a garden, but you move from one area of the garden to another one, while others move through the garden on a different path.

I found that this mirrors how people move through business offers, according to their individual needs or desires, but also, hopefully, at least somewhat guided by how your offers are placed in relationship to each other. For instance, a client of ours does an introductory course, then invites people from there into individual work with her. Or, if they aren't wanting that level of support, she has a home-study program or a small group available.

This is important, because when you sell an offer, either it's to a person who has never bought from you or it's to an existing or previous buyer. Because of the trust and relationship that has been built, it's often much easier to sell another offer to a current or previous buyer. Building trust with a new person takes time. And yes, your business must do that also.

However, if you can also invite clients along a garden path of offers, even if it's just repeating/continuing individual work, that is a great way your business can stabilize while also giving your clients the ongoing support they need.

For instance, if you're selling one-off individual sessions and you need thirty sessions a month to make your bare minimum financially, that's 360 individual people you need to build trust with and sell to in order to make your minimum for one year. That's not very sustainable, often because your business needs to build relationships with several thousand people to find 360 people ready to purchase.

Having a garden path, or having a package for clients, is *not* about extracting money from them. It's about creating a container of care. If clients are purchasing each session or each group individually, they are constantly going in and out of feeling held by you and your business. And they are forced to confront a purchasing decision at every step. This can be exhausting for everyone involved.

Instead, if you can invite folks into a container, where they know they are going to be cared for over time, then they can feel held. They only need to make one purchasing decision every so often.

What's more, if you have a garden path of offers, and you make your clients aware of this, they know they won't just get dropped when the current offer ends. This is important for them to feel held.

It's also important for them to have in their hearts the expectation of what's next. Often, I see our clients come to us with the habit of not mentioning more work to their own clients until the end of a session or series of sessions. This means that their client might have already reprioritized their time and money, so they may not be in a position to continue.

Instead, as we teach our clients, if you let your own clients know they can continue getting help with X or Y offer, then they have that in their decision-making process already.

So, for instance, you can have built into your client enrollment processes: "Because of the nature of the work, I ask clients to make an initial six-month commitment to two sessions per month. Of course, if you want to complete your commitment before six months because the work is done, or we're not working well together, you can end early. However, for most clients, that's not true. In fact, most clients end up staying for twelve months, eighteen months, sometimes two years or more because the work is so rewarding and supportive. Some do move from individual work to small group work or enter one of our other programs. If this works for you, we'll reassess every six months, or sooner if you need it, as to whether you feel complete with our work together or you need more support."

Building this in helps create continuity for the client and stability for the business.

If you need thirty sessions per month, that's fifteen clients at two sessions per month. If they each stay for a year (if that's in integrity with the work you do), then you're enrolling fifteen people instead of 360. You can see how much easier and more sustainable that is for you, and I'm guessing it will be much more powerful and impactful for your clients.

If you are newer in business, maybe your confidence and knowledge will only stretch to inviting clients to work for three months at a time. You'll design the package based on your own awareness of how best to support your clients—and this does, of course, change over time. Yet thinking in terms of packages of sessions is both beneficial for your clients and supportive and stabilizing for you and your business.

It's not just about individual client work, of course, given how many different kinds of offers there are. I'm thinking of one of our past clients who identified three different topics they wanted their clients to move through. Initially he thought that they should be put in a strict sequence, but he realized that as long as each person had a very basic understanding of the overall journey, it didn't matter what order they went in.

So, he created an introductory free video that walked them through the basics. Then, he offered three different courses over the year. One was four weeks, one was three months, and one was five months, based on the topics and depth that needed to be covered. Most people entered into the four-week or three-month course first, then took the five-month course, but not always. And graduates often moved into an alumni group or did individual or small-group work with him.

That's just one example of a creatively designed Garden Path. Each of the offers relate to each other, and they all supported the clients and provided stability to the business.

7. Selling: The process by which someone who is interested gets the information they need and decides to pay you for your products or services.

Sales, similar to marketing, is one of those necessary parts of business that most people have a huge aversion to. What I want you to know in this moment is that, like every other part of business and the world, it is founded in love and care and respect.

Sales can, of course, be done horribly, which is why so many people have come to loathe it. However, the verb *to sell* in English comes from Old English *sellan*, which simply means to give to someone what they want in response to their request. That essence, giving someone something they want because they are asking for it, is where love can be found.

In fact, the love originates even more deeply than that.

I think most people have experienced a moment in their work with a client or someone else where they were just in flow. In those moments, it feels like your gifts are being expressed in a pure way, just flowing through you. As though it's not really you doing the work at some level; you are just the conduit.

This experience led a client of ours, years ago, to ask, "If the gifts aren't really mine, if they are just flowing through me, how can I charge for them?"

The question stopped me. How indeed? Through talking to my teachers, reading Sufi texts, and being in Remembrance in my heart, I saw something quite simple and true that stunned me, and that has nourished our clients for years when they're learning sales.

The truth is that when a client shows up vulnerable and needing help in front of the business owner, the Divine gives through the heart of the business owner to the client. That is the flow so many of us have experienced.

However, what we're often not bringing awareness to is that both parties are human and have needs. A human being is never above another human being in essence. It must be a relationship of equality. We see this because the business owner is also showing up vulnerable and in need in front of the client. The finances the client has in order to pay the business owner originates with Source. The Divine is giving to the business owner, through the heart of the client, in the form of payment, referrals, and other ways clients normally give.

On a deeper level, there is not a transaction happening; you are not selling your gifts for money. Instead, what is happening is that Source is flowing to the human in both directions. You are the doorway to the Divine for your clients, and your clients are the doorway to the Divine for you.

I've witnessed how this deeper understanding of the sales process brings so much nourishment and ease.

What holds this flow is a sales process that has integrity. There's a process, a focus, a clarity that allows both sides to be present, to be vulnerable, and to build trust. We teach a process called Sacred Selling that is beyond the scope of this section, and there are many people teaching sales with integrity and heart.

What is important here is that you understand that the sales process is just that: a *process*, with a structure and a flow that your heart and your business can comfortably hold. When you understand the structure, then it is easier to work through that structure despite any emotional reactions you may have. Not by running over your emotions, obviously. Instead, you understand how a structure with integrity can help hold you steady in a sales conversation with the client. And also help you avoid sales tactics you may have unconsciously picked up that lack integrity and feel gross.

I'll share one more insight around sales. I mentioned previously in chapter 4 that I didn't really get why I was so good at sales until I connected the dots between my experience as a paramedic and the sales process. As a paramedic I had been trained and I practiced with thousands of patients, doing rapid assessments to figure out what was wrong and what solution was needed, while at the same time helping people feel cared for, safe, and seen.

Because a healthy sales process is, to a large extent, a compassionately done assessment, having that awareness makes it much easier. You are not "overcoming objections." You are asking as many knowledgeable questions as you can until the client feels seen and you understand what's needed.

Then it's easier to know if you can provide what's needed, and if there's enough of a "click" that they may want to receive that help from you. That's the essence.

When the business holds the structure of the assessment and the process of bringing a new client onboard, with all the details that entail what happens after the assessment is done, your sales can feel really enjoyable and nourishing.

We've often had clients report to us, "I never thought I would actually enjoy sales. In fact, our clients are telling us that they enjoyed the process, too."

That's the sign of a healthy sales process based in integrity and love.

8. Money: Money and finances in your business.

Money is not the only measurement of health or success in a business, but it is one of them. Money needs to be accounted for, and the business needs its own money. It starts simply with your business having its own business account and probably accounting help, especially at tax time.

As your business develops, this becomes more sophisticated, including multiple reserve accounts, like a prudent reserve (to tide you over in slow months), tax savings (for quarterly and annual tax payments), capital investment (when you need to replace big purchases, like your laptop, or bigger), and professional development (so the business can pay for any courses or mentoring you take on.)

It will also come to include bookkeeping and more sophisticated financial reports and reviews: meaning at least monthly, and maybe eventually weekly, reviews of profit and loss and balance-sheet reports, accounts receivable, and income projections.

All this may sound overwhelming and emotionally draining, which is why you get help with it.

But I want you to understand it all at a deeper level.

As discussed in the section on selling, above, when a client pays you, it's a flowing of support from Source—through them, to you. This is humbling. When we receive these kinds of gifts, we want to treat them with care.

I have so much compassion for all of us because of how dysfunctional and unjust our economic system is, and how hard it can be emotionally for many people to face their finances. While that's true, it's also true that if I'm given a gift then throw it into a corner unwrapped, uncared for, and unappreciated, that doesn't make for a very healthy relationship with those giving the gift—or how I'm able to benefit from it.

Accounting is, at its heart, very similar to how the business handles the Three Journeys of Marketing. It's how the business remains in a healthy, heart-centered relationship of love, care, and integrity with every little bit of money that flows into and out of the business. It helps you as the business owner bring care and attention to the details and the health of your finances.

Because bookkeeping and accounting are skills, like web design is a skill, it is absolutely recommended that you get help as soon as possible with them. It is a way of honoring the complexity and the details to get help, instead of soldiering on yourself, or not doing it, or doing it painfully, haphazardly, and incompletely. Unless, of course, it's one of your skills.

Maybe you soldier on alone in the very beginning. Yet I recommend this as one of the very first places you get help. It can be such a joy to have someone you trust to help you go through your profit and loss, balance-sheet, accounts receivable and income-projection reports once a month (and eventually once per week).

This willingness to be in relationship with your finances is a system that the business can hold: through accounting software, and through the support of automation and skilled professionals. This means all of your heart and attention can go into the relationship, to being with the numbers with love, rather than being drained by the struggle of managing the details with skills you may not have.

9. Support/Systems: The structures and systems, as well as additional people, that help your business run well.

I've mentioned systems, and even team, in nearly every item above. This element brings your attention to the truth that systems and team are how a business functions. The systems are, in many ways, the physical beingness and structure of your business. It's how your business has a body, mind, memory, hands, and a means of expression.

We're so used to having unhealthy systems highlighted for us. For instance, the system we've all run into when we call a large corporation and can't reach any live person—and even when we do, they often can't help, so they transfer us, and we have to explain our situation over and over. That is, if we aren't disconnected and left to start over from scratch.

Of course these kinds of painful interactions with business and organizational systems leave us upset and even enraged.

However, we are also surrounded by healthy systems. Your body has so many systems running that keep you alive without you having to think about it. Again, the circulatory system alone keeps your blood circulating throughout your body, bringing in oxygen and offloading cellular waste, as your heart beats on average 60-90 times per minute. If you had to think about and consciously cause your heart to beat every single time, as well as somehow consciously direct the cellular exchange of oxygen and waste, it would be all you could do. You wouldn't have any energy left for the beauty of life.

When you're new in business, naturally you do almost everything by hand, from scratch, as you go. This is how you develop and learn about your business, how you learn to bring your heart into all the details. It's healthy and it's a wonderful stage of development, like when a toddler is just learning to walk.

However, a healthy business, as it moves toward Momentum, cannot be supported with you doing everything from scratch every time. Systems make it possible for the business to do things on its own, without you. And, even when you are involved in the work, often the business can hold the task and hand it to you, so you need only have input at the moment it's needed (such as with the referral workflow mentioned in Third Journey Marketing above).

The same is true with team. I've found that the myth of the self-employed successful person is just that: a myth. It's extremely rare that a business can be in true Momentum and the business owner doesn't have any help at all.

It's almost required that sooner or later, as the business develops and you can afford it, you lean into the services of professionals who have skills you don't have. Bookkeeping and accounting are among the first we recommend people hire out. Web design is similar. Small amounts of administrative help, maybe between three and ten hours per month, are invaluable as you move into Stage Two and beyond.

Many businesses in Momentum never really get much beyond this size of team. Maybe a bit more administrative help, maybe some marketing support. But it's rare to need actual employees with a payroll, except for certain kinds of businesses in Stage Three and probably nearly every business in Stage Four.

The spiritual understanding here is that if you help your business develop the structures of its own beingness, you will notice a shift at some point. That shift will be when you are no longer carrying the business, but the business starts carrying you.

I remember when Heart of Business reached that stage and I was amazed. I took the deepest breath I had taken in a long time, seeing that the flow of the business was dependable. I had the support and systems in place, and there was much I no longer had to obsess over making happen. Plus, the income was dependable, month to month to month to month.

When our clients reach that phase, they often tell us of the joy that arises. When someone experiences feeling held by their business, it does initiate some realignment and healing. As they relax deeply into the solidity of their business, they often find they need to shift their source of motivation from "must work hard in order to survive" to one based in trust, inspiration, and guidance, as well as strategy. What a joyful transition that is for folks!

10. Celebration/Appreciation and Life Enjoyment.

A younger, more critical me would not have included this as an essential element of business. Older, more joyful me knows better. If you've ever been on a long journey on a straight-ish path, then you know that for every step, pedal, or mile forward, the horizon recedes by a mile. If you're focus is on the horizon, it never looks like you've made any progress, no matter how much ground you've covered.

When you're developing a business and living a life, there's always more to do. My wife Holly and I joke sometimes that the other one must be lazy because one of our to-do lists is so long. Then we realize, "Oh no, yours is, too! Ha-ha!" There's more to do in living life as business owners, parents, homesteaders, and more, than two people can really do.

Because this is true for most of us, and surely for those of us building a business, it is critical that appreciation and celebration are included in the journey. One of the benefits of working with a developmental model like ours is that there are milestones you can easily identify, even if the results of the business haven't yet changed in big, significant ways.

It's also challenging in early stages of business because no matter how well you do, it's probably still not enough to really support yourself. Your first client is sometimes a big celebration. But your fifth? Your tenth? Usually what people are focused on, understandably, is that they are still X amount short for their month's expenses, or they still have a long list of things to get done and the week is already over.

We use a structure with our clients called Compassionate Accountability. One of the components is that we alternate. Some weeks we look at what we didn't get done and learn from that. Other weeks, we look at what we did accomplish—even if little was completed or work was done imperfectly—and we celebrate what did happen.

Which brings up another question: What does celebration and appreciation look like when you are used to living immersed in criticism and "not good enough" thinking?

It takes some creativity. Often, you don't want the celebration to be extravagant or costly because you likely don't have the time or the money. Also, while some personalities like to "gamify" things and react well to rewards, many others, including me, don't.

Celebration can be simple. Sometimes just walking away from your screen, standing up, and shouting "Woo-hoo!" can do it. Sending a text to a friend or colleague, who is willing to send you a celebratory emoji back or get on a call with you for a five-minute celebration and appreciation party, can be enough. As you move forward, or for more significant things, celebration can be something simple like buying yourself a book, going out for a meal, or taking a walk in the woods at a time when you "should" be working.

For some folks, taking those breaks during the workday, making them more normal, can be one of the most impactful celebrations. It helps you learn that when you complete something, you've done enough. Even if the hours you've scheduled to be your workday aren't over yet, you can stop and ... that's it. Just stop.

Part of what's needed here is a structure, like our Compassionate Accountability. If you don't build it in, you will probably forget, like I do, to celebrate and appreciate. It can be five minutes at the end of the day. It can be a few minutes at the end of the week—or the beginning. It can come in the form of reminders that go off at certain times, asking you to stop, breathe, and appreciate/celebrate what's happening.

In fact, I'm going to pause right now and celebrate how far along I am with this book, even though it's not done yet.

It's funny: I wrote that sentence and stopped. I didn't even take my fingers off the keyboard, but I took a minute to breathe, to notice how much was done, and to feel the presence of the book in my heart and in the world. There was so much of it! That solidity enabled me to feel supported. An ease entered my heart in that moment.

That's a worthy celebration. These are the kinds of small celebrations I want you to cultivate in your business that will help your business fly. Because you're taking time to *be* with it. Because the development you are doing is real.

I encourage you to take time, maybe right now, to think about how and when you can include celebration as part of the work of developing your business.

THE TEN ELEMENTS WORK TOGETHER

Now that you've read through these ten points, and knowing you'll find even more detail in the appendix, you have a map. As you gradually put these ten elements in place more and more, and as you return to them over and over as you move through the stages of development, your business will feel, and be, more and more solid.

No model can completely and accurately depict everything needed for the journey. Your business is unique and may require a piece or pieces I haven't touched on. Yet the model I lay out here will guide you to create a solid and reliable foundation for your business. It can guide you, help you to move forward, and if needed, support you to fill in some of the gaps you might have spotted when you went through the Stages of Development in chapters 4 and 5. "What about accounting? What about systems, or team?"

Truthfully, to fully develop the elements within the stages will require leaning into these ten elements again and again.

Three Insights about Business Development

As you progressed through these points, I hope three insights occurred to you and settled in your heart.

First, I hope you've gotten a deep sense of why you need compassion and time—say, two to five years—to move into Momentum.

Second, I hope you were able to discern a natural progression of business development. The business elements naturally build over time, starting more simply in earlier stages. It's okay (even preferable) to start with unsophisticated, simple steps. Then, as the months and years go by, you circle back again and again, and it all becomes more sophisticated and advanced.

Finally, I'm hoping some rebellion arose in you. Some feeling akin to, "What? I don't want to do all of that! That's so much!"

That is a healthy response, one you can trust.

Some have more life experience with financial matters, so they find themselves putting advanced things in place quickly. Others may have a background working on teams, so they bring assistants on board earlier than others. Yet other people may see some of certain elements as unnecessary altogether, for a variety of reasons. This is your business, and you don't have to follow what I say exactly. In fact, you'll be more successful if you don't.

Use a checklist, or a strategy, or a learning from me (or anyone else) as a way of understanding the territory: of making sense of something that was vague or confusing in some way. For some, it's easier to just follow someone else's blueprint in detail. Others feel best amending a general plan or taking advice piecemeal. In any case, it's helpful to have a proven framework as a backdrop.

At some point, you're going to be making choices that are based much more on your heart than on any model. That's embracing your role as steward of your life and your business, and it's beautiful.

If you find yourself struggling with some aspect of your business, you can and should use this information as an assessment tool, to see if maybe there was something you skipped over and chose not to implement that had more importance than you had originally thought. Or maybe it's just time for that element now and it wasn't before. Or maybe you just didn't know, and now you see that it's needed.

This chapter has hopefully helped you see the pieces that you need to cycle through again and again to get a successful business off the ground and flying.

And remember, there is a detailed list in the appendix of the different pieces you'll want to consider putting in place through the Stages of Development. I encourage you to spend some time with this list. Print it out and have it somewhere handy so you can refer to it when needed.

If you're like many of our clients, it's both sobering and helpful to see that so much of what makes a small business function well is not in place. It takes away some of the mystery of why things in your business aren't running how you'd like them to. I personally experience a great deal of relief at seeing the truth, rather than just being mystified and frustrated. I hope you can lean into that compassionately, as well.

Things to Remember:
- When you see the scope of what needs to be put in place, you can understand why it takes several years for a business to reach Momentum.

- There are exceptions to everything. This is meant as a general guide. Your business may not need everything I mention. That's okay.
- At the same time, inquire into your own heart to make sure that omitting elements isn't arising from a desire to avoid discomfort.
- Many of these areas of business require the question "What support do I need to do this?" rather than the question "How do I do this?"
- You can do this. Thousands of others before you have.

CHAPTER 10

Making the Commitment

W hen you make the commitment to go "all in" with your business, what happens to heart-centered business principles? You *need* to make a certain amount of money to survive, right? And when you *must* get it all going, the temptation is to throw all the so-called niceties out the window. After all, how helpful can this wonderful heart-centered stuff really be when the pressure's on? Better to just "get real and get down to business."

I'm asking you to resist giving into this line of thought. Not primarily for moral reasons, although those are worthy of your attention, but also because it's a myth. It rarely works to disconnect heart matters from business matters, even—or especially—in terms of making money. In the rare times when doing so seems to support profit, it has painful consequences: actions that don't feel at all like you that threaten your business's message and aims; scorched-earth relationships that threaten your business's effectiveness and reputation; and more.

One of the deadliest misunderstandings in the business world is that you need to make a commitment to outcomes. Outcomes are not things to which you can commit. We have no control over outcomes, as much as we like to think we do.

In fact, the assumption that we can bend the world to our will is the fundamental misstep of business. It's not just impossible; it's also painful. It drains joy from our existence. Those who attempt it harm people, including themselves.

Unhealthy businesses think of commitment as control. The truth is that commitment is a relationship. One of the primary themes in this book is that relationships are at the heart of existence and are, in fact, the essence of what business is. Healthy and effective action arises out of healthy, respectful, and attuned relationships with self, other, and the Divine. A healthy business arises out of those healthy relationships.

Your commitment to your business is a commitment to a healthy relationship with the journey you're on. It's not a commitment to achieving a particular outcome by a particular date.

This is not to say you don't have goals, or dreams, or desires. Of course you want your business to be successful. Of course you want to get to certain levels of revenue to support yourself. Of course you want to work with goals in mind.

What I'm saying is that any commitment you might make to your business is not to an outcome. If you are planting a garden, you cannot make a commitment to growing a certain number of tomatoes. You can, however, desire, even plan for, a certain amount. Then you can make a commitment to care for the garden by tending to the soil, watering and weeding, planting a good number of plants in case some don't make it, and using tomato cages or other supports. What's more, you can love your tomato plants. Studies have shown that loving your plants—speaking to them, caring for them—has a real impact. With that love and care, the plants will then do what they naturally do: grow tomatoes. And they will be tastier and full of more nutrition than tomatoes grown industrially, without heart.

Your business is a live thing as well. It wants to develop and grow. It just needs support, care, and love. In this book I've made the effort to outline the very specific *kinds* of support, care, and love your business needs so it can grow and develop in beautiful ways. I think it's important for you to know what's being asked of you, should you decide to take on, or continue with, the task of growing a business.

To help you really get this, I want to more deeply explore a topic I touched on earlier: that your business does indeed have a heart. It has an existence that is separate from you. You are not your business, and your business is not you.

Your Business Has a Heart

According to the Sufis, everything that exists is an expression of the Divine. Every human, every animal, every plant, every rock. Everything is an expression of the Oneness.

This includes ideas and thoughts. It includes projects, buildings, and businesses. We as humans, who are Divine expressions, may have manipulated things to put together other things. But every single element used is still an expression of the Divine.

Your business, as a creation—whether it's just a nascent idea or an actual functioning business—has an existence to it. If you can talk about it as a thing, then it has that existence.

If a thing has existence, then it has that Divine connection. The Sufis call that Divine connection the "heart."

This beingness and heart of your business, is so important to be aware of. It allows you to really feel the business as something that can develop to the point where it's carrying you.

There are technical ways we can know this. For instance, when a business has a website, it's having conversations with folks when you're not present. If someone signs up through a form on your site, and they get an automatic gift by email, that's your business doing something without you. There are dozens of examples of this, including systems, like the one above, or actual support, when an assistant does something for the business and you don't have to yourself.

However, at a deeper level, it's also a way to get more information. The heart of your business is another open doorway to guidance and intuition. There are several types of information one can gain from the heart of the business.

Intimacy with Your Business

It is possible to cultivate a knowingness, an intimacy, with your business. In my experience, most people only interact with their business when they are trying to be productive: to make progress on a task or project. It's understandable from the viewpoint of our exhausting, hyped-up-on-productivity culture. But it makes no sense whatsover from a heart-based perspective.

My wife Holly and I do many things together. We work on the business, work in the garden, clean the house, cook, and run errands. You know, get stuff done. Those moments are sweet and can be very rich.

However, there are also moments, longer ones now that our kids are teenagers and we're not in motion every second with them, when we might just be sitting together, with a hot cup of something, in each other's company.

These moments open opportunities for us to share from our heart. We discuss things that are deeper, broader, and not so task-oriented. We dream. We talk through snags. And sometimes, we just sit in intimate silence, with the dog and the cat, and the boys doing who knows what in another part of the house or outside.

It's fairly rare for small business owners to take that kind of time with their businesses—to just be with them when not in productive mode. However, doing so is stunningly necessary for success. In these moments you get to know the *feel* of your business. If you take time with it, you can become aware in your own heart what the heart of the business is like.

Our clients have had all kinds of stunning insights just sitting with their businesses. They often notice that their businesses are much farther along than they thought—like when I did a double take on our boys one day and realized how grown up they were. When changes happen bit by bit, it's hard to notice how all the changes add up. But they do.

It's also in these quieter moments that other kinds of information and guidance can arise.

At Heart of Business, I ask our clients do an exercise wherein they ask the heart of their business what it wants to tell them: what it wants them to know. And also what it needs from them as the owner.

The answers are surprising. Usually what the heart of the business is asking for is very different than what the owner thinks the business needs.

"I thought my business needed me to keep working harder, to get all of this done," one client told us with tears in his eyes. "What I heard in my heart, though, was that the business needs me to rest more, to bring more lightness and fun. It really needs that."

Over and over (and over) again, I've heard similar insights arise. More fun. More rest. Let go of certain projects that aren't necessary. Trust. Know the business wants to succeed and doesn't need to be pushed. It's okay to go slowly.

Sure, I'd told them they needed to care for themselves more and not push so hard. They had heard these messages elsewhere, too. But it's hard to believe when the business isn't producing enough revenue and you have a checklist in front of you like the one in the appendix.

But when you hear this in your heart, from the heart of your business, and it resonates deep within you, it has a different impact. You can believe it. You can understand deep down how it's not just a "good idea" to slow your pace; it's actually necessary for the business's very well-being and success. The *business itself* needs it.

Then, I encourage clients to ask the heart of their businesses this further question: If you get what you need, what is it you want to give?

These answers are equally stunning. Our clients have heard (again, on a level they can feel and really believe) that the business wants to give them freedom, or time off, or the ability to care for their families, or the ability to help a good number of people, or the space to pursue their passions.

These sorts of messages are littered around the business development industry. But in those contexts, they often just sound like pipe dreams or fantastic wishes. To hear your business asking for something surprising and very specific, then hear it wanting to give you something that you yourself cherish—this exchange roots you, the business owner, in a different reality. You truly are, then, in a relationship of mutual support with the beingness of your business.

What Your Business Doesn't Have

Now, let me be clear. I am not saying your business and other inanimate objects have humanlike egos. This point arose because a client, who had been absent from the business for months while caring for a family member who had been ill, was worried she had "disappointed" her business. She was concerned that her business was upset.

My understanding and experience here, is that we as human beings have egos and personalities. We can distort the presence of the Divine within us into misunderstandings, disconnections, and drama. We can feel sad, upset, scared, and angry. This is all in the realm of personality.

This is not true for hearts of other kinds of beings, like businesses, projects, and homes. There is no ego, no personality. The heart of the presence in question is a portal to the Divine existence that thing has. There is no way to disappoint or otherwise upset your business in the human sense.

Sometimes messages clients receive from their business seem to border on interaction with a humanlike ego. One of our Learning Community members had been avoiding their business because of their own emotional pain around marketing, instead focusing on a hobby for which they had excitement and passion. The message this member heard in their heart was, "Beloved, I want your care and attention." Now, that message could be twisted, and we could project human emotions onto it. But that's not what our member felt in their heart. Instead, the message was full of compassion and love. It was a simple request, nothing more.

If you ask in the manner I'm suggesting and hear judgement or upset, you can be sure you've become entangled in your own feelings. This is understandable; it happens all the time. The remedy is to own and embrace your feelings, connect with your sincerity and humility, and listen again, more deeply.

Is It Real?

I'm sure there are folks reading this (maybe you) who have not had these kinds of experiences of communicating with the Divine heart of things. Is this all just imagination? Can these sorts of connections be trusted?

The great thirteenth-century Sufi teacher Muhyiddin ibn Arabi (more commonly called Ibn Arabi, known as al-Sheikh al Akbar, the Great Sheikh) taught that the *existence* of each thing (whether a person, sunflower, business, web page, or otherwise) is by and through the presence of the Divine Source. He also taught that the *separateness* of each thing is by and through the *hiddenness* (or *veiling*) of the Divine Source.

In other words, everything that exists comes from the Divine. Yet the only reason we can see anything as an individual thing is that the Divine presence is at least partially veiled, or concealed, within the creation of that thing. Most mystics, including Ibn Arabi, hold that if the Divine were completely revealed, everything would all melt into undifferentiated Oneness.

The reason I'm digging into this obscure mystical teaching is to help us touch even more deeply into the profound spiritual insight I opened this section with and have touched on many times in this book: namely, that each thing *is* a connection to Oneness.

You have maybe experienced moments of transcendence, of deep connection. Perhaps it was in nature. Perhaps it was when you were in love with someone. Perhaps it was just an everyday moment when everything somehow made sense or felt unspeakably good, beautiful, and right. Today and throughout history, large numbers of humans have had experiences wherein they feel and deeply know that all of reality is connected—and is somehow upheld by, in, and through love.

Due to the constraints of language and the way many of us are taught about religion, it's hard to really "get" that the Divine is not an external being—certainly not a beard in the sky. The Divine is a reality that exists within, through, without, and around everything. Furthermore, all things are comprised of this Divine reality, even though the reality is more than all things.

Just pause here. Let that sink in, if you can. Let it marinate in your heart.

The Divine is everything, an infinite Source of Love. Theoretically, and in practice, it is all accessible through your own heart. And it can be really helpful to access the Divine from different perspectives.

The Divine is both within you and outside you. You are of the Divine, yet the Divine is so much more than you. You have access to the Divine through your own heart.

The same is true of your business. It too is of the Divine, yet the Divine is so much more than your business. You have access to a different perspective/experience of the Divine through the heart of your business.

As humans, it can be easier to access various aspects of the Divine through these specific kinds of experiences, such as connecting with, perceiving, and communicating with both your heart and the heart of your business.

Is it real? As the Sufis say, you can talk and talk and talk about the water, and none of the words will replace the experience of drinking it.

Connecting with the Heart of Your Business

If you want to be led through this exercise, you can find the audio here.

www.heartcenteredbusinessbook.com/resources/heart-of-your-business

1. **Begin with the Remembrance.**

2. **Ask to be shown/to feel/to perceive the essence, energy, heart of your business.** Take your time with this. The more patient you are, the more subtlety you notice. Instead of fireworks, listen/perceive for the equivalent of whispers.

   Example: This was a bit weird for me. At first I felt silly. Then, I thought "Why not? It can't hurt," and I began the Remembrance. It was subtle at first, but I did begin to feel a presence. I could begin to feel my business as a separate thing. I felt a liveliness, an eagerness, and also it felt a little lonely, a little neglected. How strange! I can see that I've been working so hard trying to make things happen that I haven't actually been spending time with the business itself, really seeing and appreciating it. As I say this to myself, I can feel a huge sense of relief, and it feels physically as if a load was taken from my shoulders.

3. **Bring this question to the heart of your business: Is there anything it wants to communicate to you?** Hold this wondering lightly, not grasping for answers, allowing yourself to sit back and receive whatever might come, if anything. Allow yourself to be willing to be surprised.

Example: As I ask this, I can feel my doubt and skepticism come up, but hey, I want to do this. It takes a little time to settle back into my heart, to physically sit back and relax. I sense again the connection with the heart of my business, and then I get a flash of a green field, a sunny day, a sense of warmth and ease. I know in myself that this is what my relationship with my business is needing, and the business itself is asking for. Warmth. Ease. Lightness. It feels really right, and I can take a breath again.

4. **One more question, again to hold lightly, with wondering and a willingness to be surprised: If the business gets what it's asking for from you, what does it want to give, will it be able to give?**

Example: I'm so curious, and I can feel myself grasping … and then I relax, breathe, sit back. Willing to be surprised. I can feel how my business wants to grow, wants to be vibrant and full. I get a flash of that field, and how the plants in that field all just grow, with rain, sunshine, warmth. I can feel that if I can bring that to my business, my business will just want to grow and develop. This feeling goes deep in my bones, in my gut. I'm so grateful.

✿

What do you notice after spending time with the heart of your own business? Were you surprised by any part of the experience? Did it confirm things you knew or suspected, but in a deeper way? Or did you get new insights, information, or compassion?

Let it all settle in.

✿

Committing to the Journey

This chapter is titled, "Making the Commitment," but we haven't been talking about making a commitment. Until now.

The journey you're on with your business is a relationship: a relationship with your own heart, with your business, with the world. Therefore, the quality of that journey, and where you end up, is going to be largely defined by the quality of the relationships you have with each of those.

On May 29, 1999, I was staying the night with my friends Oren and Irwin, a couple who hosted me in their apartment in the Haight district of San Francisco. It was the night before the commitment ceremony between my wife Holly and me. In the Jewish tradition, the two who are to be married aren't supposed to see each other before they meet under the *huppah*, the wedding canopy.

I don't know how or why I had the courage to do this, but I went from my friends' apartment down to Ocean Beach and walked there for some time. Up until then, I had always lived my life mostly by other people's expectations. But on that night, I gave myself permission to back out, even though family had flown in and a great deal had been put into the whole thing. But it felt like too big a commitment for me to go through with just because of all that.

In a fumbling way, I spent time in my heart, remembering the previous five years of relationship we'd had together. How we'd worked through challenges, and how we enjoyed each other. I was able to commit to the journey with her, wholeheartedly, and come back relaxed and in myself, knowing I wasn't doing this for anyone else but the two of us.

I want you to feel that same sense of permission with your business. I don't want you committing to your business because you're desperate and think there's no other option. I don't want you committing to it because it's cool, or "it has potential," or anything like that. And I definitely don't want you to make an unconscious commitment, by just being on autopilot and continuing on the path.

If you've read through this book, then you have my perspective on three important learnings:

1. The long list of elements it takes for business to succeed, a general notion of the order to do things in, and the amount of time and effort it takes to get there.

2. A sense of the inner journey this will be, and the qualities you will want to be cultivating in yourself.

3. A sense of the beingness of your business, its heart, and what it truly needs from you—at least right now.

There is no way for you to truly know what lies ahead for your business, just like I had no idea of all that would occur in Holly and I's life together from 1999 until now

(September 2022 as I write this). I am joyfully committed not to an outcome but to the relationship—and to the journey. And gratefully, it's been a fantastic one.

This is not to say all relationships last this long. Some end in divorce much earlier. A client of mine is a lawyer who practices compassionate divorce and mediation. There is a way to end a journey with love and care, without struggle and fighting.

There may come a time when it becomes obvious that it's okay to part ways with your business. This commitment is not one that requires you to stick with it until you die.

However, it is a conscious commitment. You know the work. You know the terrain you'll be traveling. You know what is being asked of you.

This is the commitment you should make consciously, so you can settle in and really go for it. Or not.

The Grief of Commitment: Letting Go

Making a commitment means making space for that commitment. Taking on anything or anyone new and significant means accepting that it's going to take up time and capacity in your life. You need to let go of things to make room.

This can be challenging to face because prioritizing and letting go is more difficult than you might think.

Lots of smart people talk about prioritization in terms of letting go of unimportant or trivial commitments to make room for better ones. For example, giving up mindless scrolling on social media to take on something life-affirming, like gardening.

What gets talked about much less is this: human capacity is so limited that taking on a new commitment means letting go of other significant, meaningful commitments. There are things in your life that are important and worthy of care and attention. Nevertheless, some need to be set aside, at least for a time, in order to give attention to what you are called in your heart to prioritize.

This is not easy. It involves grief.

It will be painful to let go of commitments you care about. Because of this, no matter how excited and enlivened and clear you are about your commitment, there is also going to be grief. Sometimes it's tiny, and sometimes it's surprisingly significant.

There is little space set aside for grief in our culture—especially in my country, here in the United States. Even catastrophic grief, like the loss of a parent or child, is often not given much time or space. When one thinks about other griefs—like the grief of being ill for an extended period, or the death of a pet, or the breaking of a beloved mug—do we allow ourselves to grieve? If so, are we supported in that grieving process?

In fact, the lack of ability to process grief can often be a major contributor to stress, anxiety, and the inability to follow through. I encourage you to make more space for grief in your life than feels even reasonable. It will help you move forward in surprising ways. It will heal you.

In 2015 we moved from Portland, Oregon, to an eco-village in Danby, New York. Intentional community had been a multidecade dream of ours. We sold our house and committed to this new community we joined. It was wonderful for five years.

Through no issue with the community itself, we discovered that our life wasn't working for us. There are too many reasons, and they are too personal, to share here, but suffice it to say that we went through a tremendous grieving process leaving the ecovillage and moving to central Pennsylvania.

The grieving process was hard. Many tears were shed, and I felt the loss keenly. Until it really worked its way through my heart and being, it was hard to feel my feet on the ground here in central Pennsylvania. As the grieving has crested and ebbed, space has opened within me for deepening relationships and community where we live now.

My invitation to make open space to grieve includes grieving any commitments you might let go of in order to take on the commitment to your business. Or, conversely, if you get clear in your heart that you *aren't* going to make a commitment to your business, that will be a grief, too, since you have probably cherished dreams about it.

And yes, even deferment is worth grieving. Pain comes even when a commitment isn't being abandoned, just set aside for a future time. The loss of it from your present life is a real loss worth grieving.

Discerning the Commitment

This exercise can be done multiple times if needed. Sometimes we need to go through this kind of discernment, to open more and more deeply, until clarity firmly seats in the heart.

I have provided an audio version online in case you want to be guided through the exercise.

www.heartcenteredbusinessbook.com/resources/discerning-commitment

1. **Begin the Remembrance in your heart:** remembering the Divine, remembering the presence of the love.

2. **Ask from a place of sincerity, curiosity, and a willingness to be surprised: What is the current commitment you have been thinking you need to make to your business? What is the current commitment you are operating on?** You may not have even fully taken it on, but it's what you think needs to happen. What is it that you're seeing/perceiving/sensing about whatever commitment to your business you've been operating under?

For anything that comes up, hold it lightly, knowing that you were doing your best, maybe from a place of not being completely aware what was in your heart.

Example: It took a moment, but it hit me that I've thought that I needed to be 100 percent committed, no compromises, to the business. I've been believing that I shouldn't let anything get between me and the business, and if I do, then it will fail. That it requires unrelenting hard work ... that feels so exhausting, and yet so good to see it clearly.

3. **Ask to be shown the heart of your business, the beingness of your business, allowing it to come up in front of your heart.** Then ask in curiosity, willing to be surprised: What commitment is the heart of your business asking of you in order for it to be successful? What kind of commitment is it needing from you for this next stage of development it's in?

Example: After seeing the unconscious commitment I had to the business, it feels easier to set that aside. As I asked the heart of my business, it kind of floated up into my awareness that it knows there's a lot that needs care in my life. That the business does not need constant attention. It also does not want to be forgotten for long stretches. If I can make it one of my priorities and bring a reasonable amount of care and work to it, it will grow steadily. The commitment needed is significant, but not overwhelming or all-encompassing.

4. **As you face the commitment your business is truly asking of you, look at your life.** If you were to embrace and commit to this true commitment, is there

something you'd have to change or drop to meet that commitment? Be willing to be surprised, just asking to be shown.

Example: I can see that for my life to be reasonable, and for the business to grow, there are commitments that need to be set aside at least for a while. I can see that I might have to ask for more help from my family, my partner and kids, to help care for the house. I might have to tolerate more mess and chaos and to let my family do things their way. I can spend less time with my art this next year and bring that creativity to my business. The business doesn't want me to abandon my art but to scale back how much time I spend with it, so that the business can get the attention it needs to start to really develop. My heart feels sad about this, but I can see that it's not permanent.

5. **Holding both the commitment your business is truly asking of you, and the changes you will have to make to meet that commitment, how does that sit with your heart?** What is the authentic commitment your heart has to it all? Let go of any assumptions that you should be okay with that commitment, and let yourself be true to your own heart.

Example: It feels hard to let go of perfectionism, but it feels harder to let go of my art. That creative expression has felt like a real saving grace. And I remind myself that it's not all or nothing, it's just scaling back. My heart is actually okay with that, and there's some excitement about bringing my creativity to the business. I think I can make this commitment, at least for six months, and then re-evaluate. It feels solid, good, grown-up in a really positive way.

I would encourage you to be with whatever commitment you discerned. Grieve what needs to be grieved. Celebrate the journey you're undertaking.

✿

Things to Remember:

- A commitment to relationships is the healthy alternative to the dysfunctional commitment to outcomes that is often asked for. We cannot know how things will turn out, so the only reasonable commitment is to a relationship, not to the results.
- Your business does not have an ego, so it cannot feel abandoned, lonely, resentful, or other human emotions. Communicating with the heart of your business is another way of receiving from the Divine, the Source of love.
- Making a commitment involves grief, because there are things worthy of care and attention that may need to be set aside temporarily or permanently so you can follow what is true in your heart. The grief is real and worthy of your attention.
- Your business is asking for a very different commitment than what the culture says one must commit to a business.

CHAPTER 11

Embracing the Journey

The intention of this entire book has been to help you
deeply understand what's involved in helping a microbusiness be successful, and how to have a healthy relationship with the development of that business while remaining
in integrity and being true to your heart.

My hope is that you now feel ready for the rest of the journey—whether you're at the beginning, or, as many people
are, somewhere in the middle.

There are a few last pieces I wouldn't want you to be without. They have to do with productivity: that is, your ability
to get things done. I also want to talk about the difference
between excellence and perfectionism.

So let me start with productivity.

Choosing What to Do

In 1999, when I first started what would become Heart of
Business, I ran what I called "Success Groups." These consisted of four to six business owners who met weekly to
support one another in their business development and in

accomplishing tasks. Part of what we did in those groups was to have folks list the things they wanted to get done for the week, then come back and report the next week what got done.

In general, people only completed half or less of what they wrote down.

This has stayed consistent throughout the more than twenty-two years I've been working with clients. I became convinced early on that there was nothing wrong with people, except they were writing too many things down. We have an extremely unrealistic sense of capacity. We get done far less than we think we can.

There are many consequences to this, including a culture that makes us sick. I want to focus on two consequences in particular and to do so with compassion and kindness. Of course you are trying to do so much; there's always so much to be done! And much of it is important and consequential. I really get it. It's true in my life, too.

But *not* facing the truth of our exaggerated sense of work capacity is far from compassionate. By looking at what happens when we assume unlimited bandwidth for getting things done, we can drink in a tremendous amount of compassion and kindness for the path forward.

One consequence is that we don't have practiced muscles and clarity around setting priorities and choosing. We tend to try to do everything. What gets done then is what makes the most noise; or is right in front of our face; or seems to ease feelings of shame and inadequacy stemming from childhood trauma; or seems the most doable in view of our

EMBRACING THE JOURNEY

exhaustion; or any number of other reasons. What is truly important, strategic, or in our heart can easily get sidelined.

Because we haven't much exercised the muscle of prioritizing and choosing with deep attention to our being, our businesses take forever to develop. Wheels spin, but little movement is made. People limp along with partially developed businesses for years and years.

If you learn to accept the much more limited capacity you truly have, then you can learn to choose from the heart, with the help of strategy as a backdrop. A business takes several years to fully develop anyway. Understanding this means you can give yourself permission to lay a foundation over the course of several years. A slow build is much better than trying to fully establish your business in six months, then finding it hobbles along for ten to fifteen years due to ill-formed and/or incomplete basic elements.

I know I talked about this in the previous chapter, but I want to emphasize again the limits of capacity, the importance of choosing, and the resulting cleansing grief and clarity that comes in moving forward.

Choosing what to do (and, more importantly, what *not* to do) is, in one sense, easy. In another sense, it's very painful.

I say it's easy because with a model like the Stages of Development, and with the practice of listening to your own heart and the heart of your business, it can become relatively obvious what stays and what goes.

I say it's painful because facing the grief of letting important things go is just that. I'm being precise in word choice, here. We often use the word *difficult* in these situations, which

241

I think undermines our sense of what's involved. Choosing what stays and goes is not about difficulty. It's about grief.

One summer, I put up fencing around a little more than an acre of land (with some help from others, of course). We augured holes, placed poles, and strung fence. That was very difficult work. However, choosing to do the fencing—that is, making the decision to put it up—was easy. The hazelnut trees I was planting needed protection from deer and other critters. Putting up the fencing was a clear and obvious choice, not difficult to make in any way.

When we say, "Choosing is difficult," we're obscuring the truth of what we're facing by entangling at least two different things. On one hand, it's deeply uncomfortable, even emotionally wrenching, to go through the *grief* of choosing, which means letting go of something good to make room for your new business. On the other hand, it's laborious and sometimes exhausting to go through the *difficulty* of completing a complicated, extended project that obviously needs to be done. Both require stamina, but choosing demands a level of existential wrestling and loss that straightforward task completion does not.

By separating out the different pieces, you can more honestly and easily face and move through the whole of it. So many important decisions are avoided because grief, complication, and the choice itself are all tangled together. We unconsciously think we have to handle it all at once, so we delay the choice.

Instead, I invite to you make the choices that call to your heart, walk through the grief, and embrace the projects those choices call for.

There's another consequence to this challenge of capacity. It's depletion—sometimes to the point of illness.

Signs of Depletion

Let me tell you about another pattern I noticed in 1999 when I first began working with business owners. Clients, mostly women, were coming in seriously depleted. Sometimes their exhaustion had reached a point where the first two to three months of coaching was simply about creating spaciousness and getting rest before they could even think of moving forward.

Depletion is dangerous. So many people struggle with chronic illness from overextension. I see this mostly (but not entirely) with women, especially women of color. It's short-sighted and wrong to name it *simply* as depletion, though. This can too easily fall into victim-blaming: "If you just took care of yourself, you'd be fine!" Ridiculousness. To make it all about lack of self-care ignores the toxic productivity-obsessed culture, and the deep trauma of sexism and white supremacy, especially in the United States. Not to mention the literally chemically toxic environment in which most of us live and work. These broader systemic issues are fundamental to the depletion so many are experiencing.

These systemic issues are huge and beyond the scope of this book or my expertise to address. What I do want to name is the all-too-common habit of working too hard, as it is an issue that we as individuals have control over, and one that can have a profound effect on you and your business. It's believing the myth that we should "just do it" and get more done. We should get *everything* done. Now. We run our businesses and our lives on fumes because we have unrealistic expectations. It can be deadly.

I was leading a coaching call with members of our Learning Community, and someone mentioned they were taking an online course from someone else, a teacher I wasn't familiar with. The course's teacher was upselling from a free series into a paid series, which is fine.

Someone asked the teacher, "How much time does your course require?"

He answered casually, "Oh, like fifteen or twenty hours a week."

Pause. Deep breath. What?!

This is a *completely unrealistic* expectation. I have a business in full-on Momentum, and to write this book, I still had to be vigilant to set aside two to four hours per week to write. I could *never* set aside fifteen-plus hours per week, week after week, to take a course.

It's sadly common for people to take business development courses and make very little progress in their actual business. Often, the person teaching it has no idea how to set realistic expectations for students.

Here is an incomplete list of things people in our Learning Community have on their plates.

- Chronic illness
- Elderly, ailing parents

- Small children
- Part-time jobs
- Full-time jobs
- Anxiety
- Volunteer or activist commitments
- Past-trauma reactions from which they are still healing
- Running their business
- Friends who need help moving
- A garden, land, or animals that need care
- Adult children who are getting married
- Kids graduating from high school and going to college, needing support in the transition
- A partner or spouse who is injured or chronically ill
- Teens facing bullying
- Teens with big projects and ambitions, needing support
- Teens who don't yet drive with lots of extracurricular activities
- Teens who do drive, but how many cars can one family have?
- Friends who need childcare help or other kinds of help

Oh, and cooking? Cleaning? Taxes? Laundry?

Hopefully you don't have *all* of these at once, although many people have several at once. I, myself, have at least three or four at any one time.

When I support our community members around business development—meaning taking on things that make the business ultimately easier to run and more profitable—I suggest maybe one to three hours per week on those tasks. Or, if you're more of an immersive personality, maybe a deep-dive day once per month. Or perhaps two half days.

Regardless, I could, with a lot of planning (and a lot of support from my wife) set aside maybe ten to fifteen hours in a week—one week—to do something on top of everything else in my regular flow.

However, if anyone says you need to put upward of fifteen hours per week into their course (or other kinds of business-development effort), then they are probably living a privileged life with no real responsibility outside of themselves. That rare sort of life is fine. I imagine it's a wonderful place to be—something to celebrate. But advice meant for someone like that isn't meant to be applied to the rest of us. To attempt to do so is clearly painful.

You *can* develop your business. Your business *can* develop and grow. With steady effort, inspiration, and support, you *will* do it. But it's just not going to happen in a few weeks. Also, successfully developing a business does require a real time commitment, but that commitment can't just pile on top of everything else.

In the US, according to the Centers for Disease Control, sixty percent of adults have chronic illness. Forty percent have two or more chronic illnesses. Stress and exhaustion are big factors in illness. Conversely, rest, sleep, and spaciousness are critical factors in healing and health.

Hear this. You can't stay healthy, you can't bring your creativity, and you can't do your best work if you are trying to do too much. It may feel counterintuitive, but your business will struggle way more than is necessary, and for much longer.

But if you surrender to the reality of your limited capacity and dare to make the choices you need to make, you can move forward in measured, consistent steps that make a real difference over time.

I invite you to pause here. It's so easy to skim through this because it's probably similar to other things you've heard. However, I want to encourage you, just as I encourage our clients, to take a deep, gentle breath and allow this to sink into your being.

Embracing your more limited capacity makes for a different reality than the hard-work, twenty-four-seven "hustle" culture that late-stage, predatory capitalism has sold us. To accept your limits and insist on a healthy pace and workload is a pathway for a sustainable life. It's the path to living in alignment with your deepest heart. It's the journey that makes space for love to flourish. It's the nourishment you need to be both successful and joyful.

Four Kinds of Work

In work culture, there seems to be only one kind of project: the one where you are getting something done. It's the only kind of project given any credence. And for many of us, it's the only one that counts in our minds.

All the other tasks aren't "real" work. This assumption adds immeasurably to our overwhelm. We tell ourselves, "Oh, I only got two things done today!" when that's untrue.

It's just that all the other tasks don't count as producing something.

When I understood that there are at least four different kinds of projects—and potentially others as well—it gave me a tremendous amount of relief.

Productive Projects

Most people already know and embrace productive projects. They are the tasks we undertake which, when completed, result in something to which we can point and say, "done!" For example: the article that's written, the website that's updated, or the webinar that's completed.

Since many people fully equate work tasks with productive projects, little else needs to be said.

Communication Projects

I spend a certain amount of time every week in my email inbox (among other communication channels) and in meetings with my team. Communication is necessary: emails, text chats, phone or video calls, and in-person meetings are important parts of any business owner's workload, including mine.

Every Monday we have a team meeting at Heart of Business. In it, we share what's going on in our lives personally, we take ten minutes of silence to be in Remembrance together, then we share what's on our agendas for work that week. We also answer questions and give each other support as needed. Without this time spent communicating, the team would feel fractured, and it would be harder to really get to what the business needed from us collectively.

There is certainly a point where communication can take up too much space and keep you from digging into the things that matter. Tending to overflowing email inboxes can easily eat up half a day's work. People complain about email all the time, and yes, there's a lot of junk in there. However, many of the emails in my inbox connect me with the hearts of people I care about. My clients. People interested in becoming clients. Colleagues and other friends in my network. Maintaining that web of connection is an essential part of how our business functions and thrives.

Communication projects are valid projects. I may not be producing something myself; however, if I've met with the person who helps me with marketing, and if that meeting enables her to do something for the company, then that meeting definitely counts as work. Likewise, if I've sent twenty emails letting people know I see them and I care enough about them to offer my thoughts and input, then those emails count as work, too. The same goes for connections via social media, calls and texts, and other vital communication pathways.

GATHERING-RESOURCES PROJECTS

A lot of us have multiple projects on our plate and cannot be immediately productive with each one simultaneously. Often, we must gather resources, ideas, and information over a span of time. We collect what we need and put things in place so we can be productive later.

At other times, we need help from someone. Here the project becomes figuring out what kind of help we need, then finding and engaging the person who can best assist—whether friend, colleague, contractor, or consultant.

The incubation period leading up to the moment of productive, tangible results certainly counts as valid work. If you've undertaken a complex project, it can take many hours, days, weeks, or more to figure things out, gather resources, find people, and communicate with them if needed. A farmer would never say her spring seed purchasing and sowing aren't valid projects. In the same way, neither should you discount the time and effort you spend gathering and preparing things for later "harvest" in your business.

LEARNING PROJECTS

This fourth type of project has potential to bring a lot of freedom and fresh air to your work. When we *only* deem "productive time" as work time, we keep ourselves from experimenting and learning new things in our business.

Over the years, we at Heart of Business have seen many people want to engage with social media for their business but shy away from it because they don't know where or how to begin. I recall one client who, like many others, came to me assuming he'd need to achieve instantaneous effectiveness with his new social media efforts. This felt overwhelming due to his lack of knowledge, so he'd simply stayed away. I gave him the idea of budgeting two or three hours to start, with the intention of just playing around on the social media channel of his choice. The goal wasn't to master it quickly;

rather, to just poke around, get comfortable, look at different areas, and acquire more ease and familiarity with it.

This changed everything. The permission to be in a learning project around social media enabled this client to get truly comfortable in that space. Eventually, he found a way of engaging with it that felt good to his heart. Then he started becoming very effective as he showed up there for his business.

Interweaving Projects

When you expand your understanding of what work is, you begin to see how different types of projects build upon and weave together with each other. You can breathe a sigh of relief because you now view *all* your tasks as valid and valuable.

I remember a Heart of Business client who struggled with their own client-scheduling processes. This individual decided to undertake a learning project around figuring out what a sustainable schedule might look like. Then, having completed that, they took on a gathering-resources project, which involved researching and finding an online scheduling system that worked for what they needed. Finally, they embarked on a learning project consisting of simply playing around with the scheduling tool. They had the freedom to spend several hours with it, just learning its features and getting comfortable, without needing to be productive.

For this client, the two learning projects and one gathering-resources project took a total of about eight hours over the course of two to three weeks.

With that in place, this client was able to take on a productive project (setting up the scheduler) and a communication project (letting their clients know what it was and how it worked). They updated web pages and email templates so that it all worked smoothly. This took another four hours total.

At the end of it all, our client had a scheduling system that reduced the amount of work it took to schedule people, made their week much more sustainable, and made their life much easier and more joyful.

Embracing the four different types of work and how they interweave honors the amount of time it takes to get to the "productive project" end result. The above-mentioned client started out imagining it would take one or two hours to get a new scheduling tool. In reality, it took twelve hours over several weeks. (And, honestly, probably a bit more than that.) We still don't always see every bit of time we put into something.

When you start to see what it takes to do the work that will enrich your business in a solid and lasting way, and you start to include all four kinds of projects in your awareness, you begin to understand how long it *actually* takes to implement things. Suddenly it's clear why you have been feeling constantly ineffective and swamped. You've been overloading your schedule with too many tasks and presuming a timetable that was neither reasonable nor sustainable.

If you look at your task list now, you probably see several items you think might take one or two hours each. But in reality, each of them, like our client's "set up client-scheduling tool" project, may well take twelve hours or more and involve multiple types of projects. No wonder overwhelm happens!

I'm hoping this brings you compassion as you move forward to work on the many things required to develop your business. This is a commitment you have taken on from the depths of your heart, and it deserves to be tended with time and care. Please be kind to yourself. And know that part of that kindness means embracing the reality of the journey, so you can do it with excellence and love.

Backward Excellence

Left to our own devices, we humans often get things backward. It's not our fault. When we're in that anxious state of believing we're separate from love, we scramble to try to make things work. We scratch and claw our way toward what we think we need to be okay.

Taking on unknown, unfamiliar, or otherwise challenging projects is often a place where we end up scrambling. That's especially true if the success of the projects is related to our survival or to deep, intrinsic needs, like the ability to make a significant contribution or to receive love and acceptance.

In the backward way we approach things, we earnestly try to do our absolute best, hoping we can believe in what we did and get the chance to relax into the reality we're trying to create.

It kind of makes sense. Unfortunately, it rarely works this way. What often happens is this: a kind of perfectionism kicks in with that first step—doing our absolute best. Then, no matter how much we pour into it, it's hard to really trust that what we did is going to work. We're left feeling anxious, inadequate, and scared—no matter how much work we put in.

This can be true even when we're quite successful. Many extremely wealthy or so-called "successful" people don't have a sense of enough. They keep trying to accumulate more and more and more. Some call this greed, but I think the Buddhist idea of the "hungry ghost" is closer to the reality. Picture a ravenous apparition, with no material form, that tries desperately to eat physical food. The hungry ghost's consumption attempts never end; there is never enough. Why? Because what they are attempting to eat can never really nourish them.

In the same way, many people keep trying to "consume" task completions, goal achievements, productivity markers, or the frantic crossing-off of items on their to-do lists. But they never receive the nourishing, restful goodness they long for. There is simply *never enough*.

This doesn't create excellence. It creates the shadow of excellence, for it arises out of the traumatized, painful, soul-destroying perfectionism with which so many of us are familiar.

My Sufi teachers and my own experience have taught me that the steps to true excellence are all there. They are just backward.

Surrendering into Excellence

We're nearly at the end of this book. We've covered *a lot* of ground. There's one last piece, and then a blessing at the very end. But along with all of the things I've expressed, I want you to be overloaded with kindness and trust in yourself.

I want to share with you a Sufi teaching about excellence. My hope is that this teaching brings yet more kindness to you. Excellence can be a trap into which those of us who are at risk for perfectionism, or other forms of painful self-doubt, can easily fall.

The Sufi teaching is this: *Islam-Imam-Ihsan*. In Arabic, *islam* means "surrendered," *imam* means "faith," and *ihsan* means excellence.

As humans, we tend to take this Divine teaching and do it backward. We think we must achieve excellence before we let ourselves surrender. We think we must earn, produce, or accomplish our way into a place of trusting rest. But it's just the opposite.

Recently I had a client who was launching an offer for a program. She revealed to me that she had put into place a sophisticated, complicated launch strategy. There were free videos leading to a free online group, leading to a webinar, leading to an introduction to the paid program. Et cetera.

It was all way more complicated than it needed to be. She was overwhelmed. It had arisen out of a good intention; she wanted to fill her program with people who could really use it.

At a deeper level, though, her elaborate launch plan was rooted in a backward understanding of the Sufi teaching above. She *began* with an attempt at excellence—perfection, even—in hopes that her efforts would be successful enough to merit the trust and rest she so deeply longed for.

We've all done it. We work really hard to get something right. We pour so much into it, in hopes it won't fail—in hopes *we* won't fail. In the process, we exhaust ourselves. And we end up creating something that's much more likely to fail.

Yes, you read that right. A complicated, sophisticated launch strategy (or any business strategy that leaves you overwhelmed) means that it's unlikely to work. Why? Because no matter how good it looks on the outside, the overwhelm means you probably don't really have your arms around it. If something feels like too much, it probably is too much, and it's not likely to be effective.

There's a lot I could say about the dangers of overly complicated marketing strategies. But the focus here is on protecting your heart. I want to help you move toward a sustainable, effective excellence. This true excellence cannot come when we pursue it backward.

Here is what backward looks like:

First, we fixate on producing something amazing, effective and perfect, straight out of the gate. Fueled by a deep, fretful, even compulsive belief that *this needs to work*, we work extremely hard on it. Second, we think to ourselves, "if this is done well enough, I can trust it—I can trust it will be effective." This amounts to an attempt to generate faith or trust. Third, we believe that if all our efforts work, we can finally relax into it—we can finally achieve surrender. We can rest.

Excellence cannot arise from the fumes of exhaustion. When you try to do it this way, you'll encounter the unfortunate outcome our client did: utter overwhelm, leading to mediocre or painfully small results, leading to the destruction of faith, leading to no space to rest.

Sometimes folks *are* successful using a backward approach. However, if the ultimate faith and surrender aren't there from the outset, there's no true rest. The nourishment you seek cannot come while you're locked into patterns of perfectionistic overwork, clinging to a small scrap of faith that someday, rest and enoughness might arrive.

It's no way to work. It's no way to live.

With kindness, let's try it the other way—the way it's meant to unfold.

Starting with Surrender

Starting with surrender means leaning into vulnerability.

When you meet someone, you can't really have an abiding faith in who they are until you've come to know them. Over time, you learn of their integrity, care, and attentiveness. To gain that faith, you do have to take a risk. You must come close to them and open yourself up. We undertake this kind of vulnerability cautiously, especially if we've been hurt, and that is just good sense. I'm not advocating that we all fling ourselves into vulnerable positions with people or things. It's okay to go slowly. It's good to test the waters and listen to one's intuitions and cautions.

But ultimately, if you are going to have an excellent relationship, you must first be vulnerable in order to come close. For how else can your faith in the other person develop? The relationship with the person can then become excellent because you can focus on actually being with them. Vulnerability brings about a closeness that allows you to leave behind the cautious, testing, trust-developing stage.

Remember the client with the complicated launch strategy? In that session, I helped her reverse directions and begin with surrender. She became vulnerable about her sincere desire to help and her willingness to show her heart to (and connect with) her audience. She also became vulnerable about her limited capacity and skills. These were deep forms of surrender. She let go by accepting her "enoughness," and also by realizing that she can't force an outcome. Even with the world's most sophisticated launch strategy, she still can't make people buy.

This surrender can feel scary, and that's appropriate. But it can also bring deep relief. There is a beautiful freedom that comes when we stop trying so hard to control and manage outcomes, and simply come into alignment with what is.

From there, it's easy to see faith begin to bloom. You see people in your audience respond to your caring and sincerity. You begin to trust your own expression of that care, as well as your creativity in it. And you're willing to show up more and more, to be visible to your audience, as your faith in yourself (and in them) grows. You are no longer striving to manufacture sales; you're opening yourself to authenticity, love, and hope.

Our client with the elaborate launch scheme ended up scrapping the complicated model and taking on something much simpler. Her new strategy involved creative, caring, and clear messages that extended empathy to her audience. In her communications, she also expressed a strong desire to help and a genuine belief in her program to be one way for people to get the support they needed.

She courageously sent those messages out on a regular basis—even when it made her feel nervous, vulnerable, and like she had less control of the outcome. Her words from the heart went out by email and social media. People responded, and she connected with them.

This time, the surrender with which she began, and the faith—the *imam*—and trust that grew within her, meant that she had real solid ground under her feet and heart. That inward security and confidence allowed her to express the excellence—the *ihsan*—in her heart and mind. She did so without doubt, without holding anything back.

And you know what? Where initially there were hardly any responses to her overly sophisticated launch strategy, now, with her heart present and a much simpler strategy, her program filled, and she had the honor of interacting with a delightful group of people—all of whom she truly helped.

Now, this approach doesn't always guarantee a positive, money-filled outcome. Our client had done hard work prior to her new program launch. It wasn't simply about learning to be more vulnerable. She also worked to become clearer in herself about her messaging and to put other pieces in place that gave her business a firmer foundation. And previously, she had worked hard to gather an audience.

You can't operate solely on surrender and faith. You need knowledge, too. Business strategy is just that: knowledge. It's not wisdom, although it can be an ingredient in wisdom. It's not love, although it can be a vehicle for love. And it's not excellence. Excellence blooms out of your own heart's relationship with what you care about.

There's More

You're somewhere on this journey. Maybe at the bare beginnings, just wondering about starting a business. Maybe you're deep in it, wrestling with all the challenges that come with the middle journey. Or perhaps you're at a much later stage, wondering how your business is going to evolve and deepen.

But for now, this is enough. You are enough.

Hopefully this book has given you the compassion and kindness you need to believe in your own enoughness. Hopefully it's helped you deepen your trust in your own heart. Hopefully it's given you a roadmap you can trust, so you know the terrain across which you're traveling. Hopefully it's provided what you need to take the next gentle steps forward.

I'm so grateful to have you on this journey with me—and with all of us. This world is hurting. So many beings are hurting. We've inflicted great harm on each other in the seeking of financial profit. We've devastated the environment and cultures, and we've lost some of our most precious connections: relationships of love and justice with land, ancestry, creatures, and peoples.

Our hearts ask, "Is love available even here?"

I know it is. Love is always available. It's how we travel in this world.

The Sufi saint Rabi'a of Basra once said about people of faith, "Some people worship You out of fear of the fire, and if you keep them from the fire, they are happy. Some people worship you out of desire for the garden, and if they are in the garden, they are happy. I do not worship You like this. I don't care if I'm in the fire or in the garden, I only want to be near You."

We don't know how this story ends yet. There is great hope, and there is great cause for concern. If we travel with love—with surrender, faith, and excellence—then our hearts can be at peace. At the same time, traveling with love gives us the best chance of helping our greatest hopes to come to pass.

Things to Remember:
- At the heart of everything is love. Everything is an expression of the Source of love, including your business and everything related to it.
- Your business is worthy of care and attention. If you are bringing your heart and love to it, it is also a small but significant part of the healing our world needs.
- To reach excellence in anything, including your business, you start with surrender, which moves you into an experience of faith and trust. Excellence

arises when you are standing on the firm ground of faith and trust.

- We need each of us to be the ground for each other, to lift each other up. If anyone is missing, we are not whole.

A Blessing

The very last thing I want to give you is a blessing. Blessings, like all things in this world, need to be given and received consensually. If you don't like the idea of a blessing, please allow me to wish you well.

Whereas much of our work in the field of business development is workshop-style exercises, spiritual practices, including blessings, are different. We do the practice, then the practice itself does the work. You can be carried. You've probably felt it at different moments in your life. I hope this blessing helps you to feel carried.

A blessing in my tradition is an actual thing. It is a form of intercessory prayer that asks for the Divine in all its forms—this may include angels or other extensions of the Source—to come to the aid of the person receiving the blessing so that they can be supported and carried.

Here is the blessing in written form. And, if you like, there's a link to a video of me giving the blessing.

www.heartcenteredbusinessbook.com/resources/the-blessing

Audu bilahi mina shaytan ir-rajim

Bismillah ir-rahman ir-rahim

In the Name of the Oneness, most merciful, most compassion-ate, most kind,

We ask You, from whom we are not separate in any way, for there is no "other" to ask.

Please send Your love, and care, and justice, and beauty upon this beloved.

Help this holy beloved to know that their heart is always cared for, that their every step is already guided, that they need do nothing alone.

Help to open the way, to reveal the path, to make the signs unmistakable.

Shower upon them nourishment, and support, and care in abundance.

Help all of those who need the gifts this beloved has been given, to find their way to them, without blocks, or veils, or hesitations.

Please help this beloved, that their provision comes to them with ease and grace and joy, that they may be of service to those they are best suited to support.

May we all be the earth for one another, supporting each other on the path of love.

Amin. Amin. Amin.

Business Development Master Checklist

Let me begin by naming the obvious: this checklist can feel a bit overwhelming. There's a lot on it. Specifically, there are more than 110 different items on it, and it's still not completely comprehensive.

However, it's also meant to encourage self-compassion. When you see the checklist, you'll understand more deeply why it's true that you can't fully develop a business in just six months. It usually takes three to five years of focus on business development to get your business into Momentum.

Hear this, though: it's all absolutely doable. None of it is rocket science. And don't worry about the elements that seem more difficult or expensive. You'll be able to get help with them, especially as your business develops. In particular, the more costly elements don't show up until later in the developmental stages when your business will be able to afford them.

You can download this checklist or copy it from the book. I want to walk you through each of the items, though, so you can understand them. Some of the language here is specific to Heart of Business concepts, so it's helpful to have some guidance to know what is meant.

The checklist is organized by the stages of development, which we covered in chapters 4 and 5. Further, each stage has ten categories. As you move through the checklist, you'll see each category develop. You won't touch some categories at all in certain stages; either you'll have completed them at an earlier stage or you won't need them until a later stage.

You can follow this link to get the downloadable version of the checklist.

www.heartcenteredbusinessbook.com/resources/master-checklist

The Ten Elements of Business

1. Business Foundations: These are the elemental pieces your business stands upon.

2. Website and Social Media: Even if you hate social media, nearly every business needs some way for folks to find them on the internet. You don't have to pursue a social media strategy.

3. First Journey Marketing (Becoming Known): How your business reaches new people.

4. Second Journey Marketing (Nourishing Those Waiting): How your business deepens relationships of trust and care with your current audience.

5. Third Journey Marketing (Supporting Referrals): How you support your clients, colleagues, and larger network to refer people to you.

6. The Garden Path: The offers your business makes, and how they relate to one another and support repeat business. Sometimes referred to as the business model.

7. Selling: How you handle the process by which someone who is interested gets the information they need and decides to pay you for your products or services.

8. Money: How you handle money and finances in your business. This includes bank accounts, bookkeeping, and accounting.

9. Support/Systems: The structures and systems, as well as additional people, that help your business run well.

10. Celebration/Appreciation and Life Enjoyment: Rest, joy, connection, and self-care are critical parts of a well-running business. They need to be on a checklist or else they get forgotten—which undermines your business and, ultimately, your health and well-being.

Creation: The First Stage of Development

Remember, this First Stage of development is just getting the very basics in place and learning who your business really is in the world. Ideally, one spends less than six months in this stage. But, depending on life circumstances, sometimes six months isn't possible. If you're working a job or you have young children or other responsibilities, you might spend a year in this stage. It's all okay.

Business Foundations

☐ Cultivate awareness of your Jewel: Your Jewel is the inner sense of uniqueness, beauty, and power that your heart carries. It is a spiritual element in your heart. Notably, you won't necessarily know your Jewel well; it can take years of spending time with your own heart to *deeply* know it. However, unearthing your Jewel and beginning to embrace it is a big opening for many people.

☐ Craft your One Compelling Sentence (OCS). Your OCS is your brief, conversational, non-marketing-language way to say what you do. The OCS is the Heart of Business term for one sentence that is meant to help folks know if you are relevant to them. It doesn't go into detail about what you do; it's really all about them.

☐ Write your Customer-Focused Story (CFS). Your CFS is a more in-depth story of your business that you use as a template in marketing. The CFS is the Heart of Business term for a five-element message built on what we call "marketing syntax." In non-manipulative, non-exaggerated, non-egoistic language, your CFS helps make what you do approachable and understandable. It's a template that can then be used later for your website, for sales pages, and for content creation. It's a touchstone. Clients have used it as the outline of a book and as a way of helping their team and their clients clearly understand what they do and who they serve.

Website and Social Media

☐ Set up a basic website. Your site should contain an opening message, your One Compelling Sentence, and your Customer-Focused Story as it develops. Very often, this version of the website is created for free or extremely low cost, being just good enough. It doesn't need to be beautiful, and it doesn't need to represent you perfectly. It can feel impossible to be in business without having something of a website, and this is the answer at this stage.

☐ Be present on one social media platform. Experiment with connecting, posting, and being visible. So many folks are already active or semi-active on a current social media account because that's where they maintain contact with their people and their community. Because that's true, it's the beginning of where your business can show up also. Social media presence, at this stage, need not have systems or sophistication.

First Journey Marketing: Becoming Known

☐ Work through initial neediness and fears about being visible and taking up space.

☐ Begin to reach out to new people you may have heard of but don't know yet. These are folks that are still near to your existent social or professional circles.

Second Journey Marketing: Nourishing Those Waiting
☐ Work through initial neediness and fears around speaking up and taking a stand.
☐ Find your voice, then start to develop your position, opinions, stance, and speaking it to your audience. At this stage it's experimental, perhaps even sloppy, and not very consistent. That's okay.

Third Journey Marketing: Supporting Referrals
☐ Work through initial neediness and fears around asking for referrals.
☐ Find clarity about what you are asking referrers to do, and when and how to invite them to refer folks to you.

Garden Path
☐ Craft your first, most nascent, most basic offer. It will be simple and non-comprehensive. You do not yet need to think strategically about further or more complex offers.

Selling
☐ Identify questions to ask to get to know a potential client's situation. At Heart of Business, we call this the Client Questionnaire. It's less in-depth than a true intake session (as some health practitioners do), yet enough for you to discern whether you can help.

☐ Establish resonant pricing for each offer. Resonant pricing is setting a price that feels good to your heart. We teach a somatic and heart-based approach to setting prices. The important thing is that you feel comfortable saying your price, regardless of what others think you "should" charge.

☐ Make your "after 'yes'" details clear, with consistent paperwork and flow for brand-new clients.

☐ Work through neediness and issues around sales.

Money

☐ Face and work through neediness issues around money / income.

☐ Separate business and personal accounts from each other, each with subaccounts, such as "vacation," "taxes," and "prudent reserve."

☐ Identify inexpensive (or free), non-extravagant celebration and fun around money.

Support/Systems

☐ Set in place a contacts / database system. Your business will eventually hold far more relationships with people than you could hold in your personal life. Beginning to use a very basic contact system allows the business to start to remember people and pertinent parts of their information.

☐ Make an information sorting or filing system. You're starting to create materials for your business, such as marketing messages, offers, and other pieces. You'll need some basic way of organizing and storing this information so it can be easily found again.

Celebration/Appreciation and Life Enjoyment

☐ Develop a habit of noticing and appreciating successes on a weekly basis. It's important to cultivate awareness of your small successes, especially at this stage where results aren't going to be huge. Otherwise, it might feel as if you are putting in a lot of work and not getting anywhere.

☐ Start to identify your capacity or "enoughness." Because you are at the beginning of the journey and there are several years of work ahead to get to Momentum, the list of things to do can seem endless. You may also have excitement from being new in business, so you feel fine working a *lot*. This is a time to be cautious and start to recognize enoughness and capacity. It goes hand in hand with noticing and appreciating successes because it allows you to say, at the end of a workday or week: "I did enough. Of course I haven't arrived anywhere significant yet, but I can see that I did work and made progress. I can rest."

Pause before Continuing

For some, reading this list will be no big deal. Maybe you've been involved with setting up a business before, so it seems familiar. Or perhaps your nervous system is simply set up to more easily handle such a long list of to-dos. If this true for you, you can jump right to the Second Stage list below.

For others, the above list may feel impenetrable, overwhelming, or activating in a bad way. Or you may be the kind of personality who sees something like this and unconsciously starts to figure out how to implement it all immediately.

If you find yourself adversely affected in some way, please pause here. It's okay. Really, it is.

Please know:

- Help can be found with all these items. For every task you find difficult or overwhelming, there is someone else for whom it's easy. You no doubt do things with ease that others would find difficult.

- The First Stage items are not meant to be implemented in a week or even a month. It all takes time. Again, most folks spend at least six months creating and establishing their new business.

- The list above should be read as a collection of general guidelines. People go through business creation in all kinds of ways, with all kinds of adaptations and changes to match what they need.

As we continue, know that some items will get more complicated and/or sophisticated. The second and Third Stages take several years to implement, often (indeed, usually) with help from others.

So read the list above (and the lists below) as you would a map. Just because you're looking at a mountain range doesn't mean you have to be climbing right now, or this afternoon. I've watched thousands of different people work successfully through these checklists in various ways. Many freely adapt them, and many find support to work through them.

I can say with confidence that you've got this. You really do.

Concentration: The Second Stage of Development

Stage Two is about expanding on the solid foundations of Stage One, including making your communication clearer, expanding your reach to more people, more fully implementing the Three Journeys of Marketing, deepening relationships, and generally seeing your business develop into something that feels like a real business.

It's exciting but demanding; there's a lot to do. Overwhelm often happens in this stage, not because the business is broken or anything is wrong with you, but because the business is starting to really work. Please be kind to yourself. Remember that getting fully into Stage Three: Momentum takes most people three to five years. Lean into the five heart qualities from chapter 8 and you'll get through this just fine.

Business Foundations
☐ All handled in the First Stage.

Website and Social Media
☐ Develop a more effective website—what Heart of Business calls the "Basic 8." These are the basic pages you need to connect with new visitors.
☐ Maintain a modest design budget. The business is still evolving, and the revenue is not completely solid and

predictable. This is not the time for the hugely expensive website or logo. Yes, you can step up and make something more beautiful and more functional. Just be mindful.

☐ Set up a subscription form that captures email addresses and adds them automatically to an autoresponder.

☐ Create a free giveaway for new subscribers.

☐ Create an online sales page for each offer. The page may lead to a "buy" button in some cases. For other offers, like an individual session package, it will lead first to an inquiry form.

First Journey Marketing: Becoming Known

☐ Reach out not just to new people, but also to hubs, influencers, and strategic alliance partners who can make you visible to their audiences. This would include offering content for their audiences, which could be written or recorded content, or live content such as interviews, guesting on podcasts, or webinars.

☐ You may start to experiment with social media advertising. Caution to not get caught up trying to create sophisticated ad-to-webinar funnel structures, like those discussed in chapter 5.

Second Journey Marketing: Nourishing Those Waiting

☐ Make clear decisions about publishing content to your audience, including format and frequency.

☐ Publish consistently according to those decisions.

☐ Begin to build up a library of content, in whatever format, to aid in Search Engine Optimization (SEO). This will help support further First Journey Marketing.

Third Journey Marketing: Receiving Referrals
☐ Establish a clear system and workflow for requesting referrals from clients, so that referrals take place with regularity and consistency.

Garden Path
☐ Create new offers that start to leverage your time/ capacity. In the Concentration stage, you move beyond having just one or two simple offers. You start to think about larger offers, like courses or groups, that can be supported by your growing audience.
☐ Pay attention to sequencing: in other words, how offers lead into each other to support repeat business.

Selling
☐ All handled in the First Stage. It can be good to circle back through the pieces again, make your process more effective, settle into it more deeply, and celebrate what you've accomplished.

Money
☐ Institute a "Pay Yourself First" system. "Pay Yourself First" is an approach we teach at Heart of Business wherein you, as the business owner, are included in

the expenses of the business. You aren't just paid with whatever is "left over" at the end of the month.

☐ Set up financial accounting systems. This includes not only regular accounting, but also starts to include accounts receivable: tracking people who have committed to pay you but haven't yet. This system allows for reasonable income projections into the future, so you can start to think about and plan for cash flow beyond the month you're in.

☐ Get help with accounting and bookkeeping. A bookkeeper and an accountant are usually the first outside help (except maybe a web designer) we recommend to our clients. This task is usually emotionally burdensome. And it's necessary, obviously, to avoid getting into hot water with tax agencies. It just makes sense. Hiring help in these areas also allows you to start to plan for not just taxes, but also other expenses. When the work is already done by someone else, then you can more easily spend regular time (hopefully weekly, but no less than monthly) reviewing the financials and keeping an eye on the financial health of your business.

☐ Find a merchant account to more easily process online payments. Move beyond a simple button from a common service like PayPal to using a more sophisticated online shopping cart service, and offer more options for payment.

☐ Save and account for taxes. In addition, begin to set aside other savings for other purposes. Examples include a prudent reserve (to cover expenses in slow times), capital expenses (bigger purchases like replacing your computer), and a professional development fund.

Support/Systems

☐ Put in place an autoresponder to handle newsletter and email subscription automation. If your business is building an audience through an email list, you need an autoresponder/email broadcast service that can handle someone subscribing or unsubscribing, as well as delivery of anything you want to send them.

☐ Establish a project/task management system. Here you graduate from lots of to-do lists to a more organized way of tracking projects and tasks. This can include ways to capture tasks that repeat or tasks that will happen in the future for which you need reminders. As well, the system can include templates for entire projects that can easily be repeated. There are many different online systems to do this. While none of them are perfect, it's important to find one that closely matches how you naturally work.

☐ Set up an information system: in other words, a way of organizing information that you accumulate in your business that you'll want to be able to access easily in the future. Examples here include outlines for classes and workshops you wish to repeat; job descriptions you used to hire assistants; articles and other content you offered to your audience; and workflows and checklists you used to complete projects. This is part of the memory of your business, so you don't have to hold it personally.

☐ Begin to experiment with outsourcing to a team (e.g., a web designer, a virtual administrator, or perhaps others). It's unlikely at this point that this would mean an employee on payroll. Rather, we encourage our clients to hire virtual assistants and contractors to begin to experiment with how to use someone else's help in your business before you desperately need it. Even if it's just one to three hours per month to handle posting content you've written, or some other small task, it gets you used to the idea of getting help. It also teaches you how to communicate with an administrative assistant if you don't have that experience yet.

☐ Start the process of systematic task delegation. This is related to the point above, where you start to learn how to hand off tasks in a way that is effective and respectful. There is a learning curve to this. You don't want to just dump stuff onto an assistant because it provides instant relief from your overwhelm; or micromanage an assistant because you're worried it won't be done perfectly; or fail to communicate in a timely and clear manner with an assistant because you get caught up in other things or don't know how to explain what you need. Such actions annoy the assistant, of course. But they also don't really free you up in any way. Delegation is a skill, and it can be learned and practiced.

Celebration/Appreciation and Life Enjoyment
☐ Learn to consistently define "enoughness" in a project and know when to stop. This is critical. By now, you've

begun to see the iterative nature of business development. You're realizing you will return to many parts of your business over and over to keep making them better as you learn more and progress forward. This also means you can start to develop a sense of when you have done enough—when the project is complete for the moment. Or, on a smaller scale, when you've done enough in a day or a week. Enoughness means you can walk away, leaving a task in process, and take time off. This is a critical part of life, as well as being an entrepreneur. No one else, except maybe friends and loved ones, is telling you to stop. You need to give yourself this gift, this task, this permission, of calling it "good" for now.

☐ Define work boundaries. Related to enoughness above, start to create a healthy work-life rhythm and schedule. This keeps you from overscheduling clients on free time and working night and day without respite. This is about creating a sustainable, healthy rhythm of living, which includes significant downtime.

☐ Make downtime for rest, relaxation, and fun. These things can happen on a daily, weekly, and monthly basis. It can be easy to use downtime in ways that aren't really nourishing. So establish the support and awareness you might require to make sure you actually enjoy your time off—doing things you love and spending time with people you care about. Yes, fun and relaxation can happen during the work week. We at Heart of Business love to see our clients do that. At the same time, having rest and fun happening outside of designated work time is also important for your nourishment.

☐ Schedule social time with friends, family, and loved ones on a weekly and monthly basis. We all have different needs around this. Some are more introverted, and some are more extroverted. Regardless, we all do need at least some connection with others. Bring in an awareness of that need, and make sure you get that connection time, to whatever level is supportive for you and your heart.

Momentum: The Third Stage of Development

Entering Momentum means you start to address the painful feast-and-famine cycles that commonly appear in Stage Two. The more that your business develops into Momentum, the more significant and predictable your revenue becomes, and your confidence and clarity about the business deepens.

You'll be putting into place systems and support, as well as settling into your own voice. Your offers through the business start to shine, and your experience with what you do really shows.

The items in the checklist below presume that the pieces from the First and Second Stage checklists (above) are set firmly in place.

Business Foundations
☐ All handled in the First Stage.

Website and Social Media Presence

☐ Develop a more sophisticated social media presence, if you're using it. Either expand the number of channels on which you are present, or make more strategic use of the content you've been creating on a single channel. These things can happen as you have more administrative help, for it becomes quite challenging to show up in multiple places without feeling scattered.

☐ Consider doing some social media advertising as part of your First Journey Marketing and integrate it with your website/online presence. Although you may have started to experiment with this in Stage Two, now you really want to make it work. The key here isn't necessarily the advertising per se; rather, it's a focused, effective way to have your business show up in front of many new people without overwhelming you. Here you just turn it into something that happens consistently.

☐ Make resources easily available on your website for clients, to make access to supplemental materials much easier. In Momentum, your website develops to become more than just a place where new people begin to engage or others sign up for offers. It develops into a resource for current clients and participants, making it much easier and more sustainable to give support to larger numbers of people without effort.

First Journey Marketing

☐ Institute systems to easily deliver strategic-alliance content. Similar to the second item in the Website and

Social Media Presence section just above, your First Journey Marketing has systems and workflow, probably supported by administrative help, to get your business in front of new networks, communities, and organizations.

☐ Generate a list of potential people, communities, organizations, and businesses to research and contact over the next six to twelve months. Networking has become less about individual clients, and more about connecting to what Tad Hargrave from *Marketing for Hippies* calls "hubs": people who have positions of trust and influence within a network. Connecting with hubs helps you be seen by entire communities rather than one by one.

Second Journey Marketing

☐ Have one to two months (or more) of topics/ideas in reserve, or even pre-created.

☐ Schedule an editorial/publishing calendar that loosely or closely matches your schedule of offers and promotions. At this stage, your ability to share your expertise and experience with your audience becomes very consistent, easy, and supported.

Third Journey Marketing

☐ Put a system in place to wow clients with little extras/nice touches. You might have done this a bit by instinct in the First Stage of development. Now your business has structures, resources, and supports to be able to really share extra touches of care to clients you're supporting.

Sending gifts on client birthdays or holiday cards are examples of this.

☐ Provide a list of potential referral sources to research and contact over the next six to twelve months. Similar to contacting hubs/influencers, this means having the system and workflow of finding and researching potential referral sources, so you can reach out to them and make a connection with both integrity and ease.

Garden Path

☐ Set a strategic sequence and flow to your offers, to the extent possible. Not every offer will be linked and lined up with other offers. Still, it's helpful if your main offers are connected in some way. This helps people come back.

☐ Leverage your offers according to your time and work capacity, and do so in such a way as to not create income ceilings lower than desired. This requires work with the business model so that you have the revenue and profit you need, while maintaining a schedule that you love.

☐ Gain clarity on how prospects/clients move down your Garden Path. This is related to the first point: that not only are you clear with how the offers are connected, but your clients are too. You have a process in place that supports them moving from one offer to the next, provided it's in integrity with what they want and need.

Selling

☐ All handled in the First Stage and potentially deepened in the Second Stage. Check in again with your process, and definitely celebrate any solidity, effectiveness, and ease here!

Money

☐ Build up a prudent reserve. Often, this is designated as four to six months of business expenses saved in reserve. You are building toward this steadily.

☐ Build up a vacation reserve in addition to the prudent reserve. The prudent reserve is for unforeseen dips. The vacation fund is to support conscious time off without taking a hit to income. It can be whatever feels sustainable to you: sometimes two to four weeks of expenses, plus the expense of the vacation / time off itself.

☐ Build up a capital expense reserve. This is an account set aside for periodic reinvesting in your business. Examples include updating your laptop every so many years; buying video equipment if you do video as part of your marketing; paying for the cost of administrative help during a transition to a newer, more sophisticated system; and updating or redesigning your website every few years.

Support/Systems

☐ Put in place a "just enough" team. For some businesses, this might be quite minimal, such as a modest number of hours from a virtual assistant, a bookkeeper and accountant, and a web/online-presence person who can help update and troubleshoot problems. For others, it might be more extensive, but at this point it rarely encompasses a full-time paid team on payroll.

☐ Gain more systematic clarity on how to delegate. At this stage, business owners have usually picked up the skill of delegation to some extent. But you may want to further hone this skill so you have more ease handing tasks off in a way that works for your team and gets things done.

☐ Develop your leadership capacity. Without needing to take on what might be considered full-blown leadership development, you can still cultivate qualities for communicating vision and supporting your team so that people are happy and effective working with you.

☐ Prioritize business projects/tasks for handoff as revenue covers more support. As the founder/owner of the business, decide your own ideal capacity and focus. As your sense of this deepens, more and more tasks and projects can be handed off to team members, preventing you from getting caught in business details that drain you, slow you, or otherwise don't feel nourishing.

☐ Some Stage Three businesses may want legal support to protect intellectual property and to be aware of other business-related legal issues.

Celebration/Appreciation and Life Enjoyment

☐ Fine-tune your schedule for real enjoyment, such as regular three-day weekends or other modes of spaciousness. When a business starts humming in Momentum, a business owner can often feel like they are "getting away" with something because suddenly three- and four-day work weeks, with plenty of income, become more regular. Claiming that, and supporting your team to have sustainable schedules, brings so much enjoyment.

☐ Plan for vacation time. Have vacation time in your calendar, and plan your offers around vacations so you get time off.

☐ Add in "extras" for your team/support staff to invest in their happiness and well-being. Support your team in enjoying their lives as well.

☐ Bring beauty and ease into your workspace. Move past mere functionality, bringing in art or objects of beauty that help your workspace be nourishing as well as functional.

Stage Four: Independence

As mentioned previously, this stage is completely optional. Most business owners find that what they really want is a high-functioning, profitable Stage Three business. The benefits of Stage Four include having a business that can be sold or handed off, that can function well without your presence for long periods of time, and that can impact many more people than a Stage Three business typically does.

To be successful transitioning into this stage you must be prepared to take several years doing so, to learn new skills involving becoming a leader and CEO, and to turn your focus away from doing the work with clients toward the work of developing a company. This stage takes resources, money, and time because often things need to be put in place before there's the revenue to fully cover them.

A general caution on most of these items, especially the marketing and systems items, is to know how to preserve and deepen a sense of real presence, love, and care, while scaling to reach and serve significantly more people. The owner/leader needs to not lose sight of what's most important during this kind of expansion and development.

Business Foundations
☐ Business foundations may need to be reworked to make sense for an organizational identity, one that isn't necessarily tied to the presence of the business owner.

Website and Social Media Presence
☐ Often the website needs to be retooled to represent an organization and not just an individual. Language and presentation need to match a newer, larger identity beyond the personal.
☐ Sophisticated website systems may need to be implemented, including Learning Management Systems or platforms for delivery of offers and other sophisticated back-end functionality. There may be more advanced applications also, on the front end, to support marketing.
☐ Social media or other online presence needs to walk carefully between preserving real human presence and interaction and also being able to expand to reach many more people.

First Journey Marketing

☐ Predictable systems and strategies to reach much larger numbers of new potential clients will need to be implemented, without losing the business's heart.

Second Journey Marketing

☐ Truly consistent, personal, useful content needs to be produced. Depending on the intentions of the owner, it may become a priority to introduce other voices as well so that the audience develops trusting relationships with the organization and not just one person.

Third Journey Marketing

☐ Conscious and engaged systems of supporting referrals, supported by the team, will help expand reach into new communities.

Garden Path

☐ The quality of the offer and of the delivery of that offer becomes more than rock solid, holding up well even when the founder is not the one delivering the offer.

☐ Often the number of offers is simplified, and they are clearly connected to each other to make as clear as possible a pathway for the clients/customers.

☐ Individual work, if offered, is mostly done by trained/ mentored practitioners.

☐ A practitioner training program may become part of what's offered, generating revenue to support the training and mentoring of potential contractor practitioners.

Selling

☐ More sophisticated systems and processes may need to be put in place. Measuring how effective sales are, having more people than the owner involved in the sales process, and in some cases removing the owner from the sales process, will become important.

Money

☐ The equivalent of a chief financial officer is hired. For many tiny Stage Four businesses, this may be a very skilled bookkeeper who has good communication skills. The owner/founder meets weekly with the CFO to keep an eye on the numbers, carefully tracking accounts receivable, projections, and cash flow.

☐ Payroll for employees is put in place.

☐ Benefits for employees are put in place, as well as legal support for making sure you handle issues around employment without accidentally doing anything illegal.

☐ Building in bonuses or other forms of profit/revenue sharing for the team.

Support/Systems

☐ Legal support will be important. If you have employees, contractors, intellectual property, trademarks, and so on, all of these require legal support.

☐ You will need to get clear on what size team is necessary for the business. It's easy to both underhire, trying to save money, and overhire, trying to get too much support (or too high a level of support for what you actually need). Some systems around hiring will be important.

☐ Decision-making systems and flow will become critical. As more people are involved, decision-making can get bogged down, and that can undermine flow.

☐ Clarity around organizational culture: How do you communicate vision and values when it's more than just you, so that everyone who comes to your company is cared for the way you want them to be?

☐ Project management becomes an important skill to have on the team somewhere, so that projects involving more than one person, or handoffs between team members, happen with care and attention.

☐ In general, every system needs to be sophisticated, rock solid, and able to be used by a team so multiple people can access it.

Celebration/Appreciation and Life Enjoyment

☐ Celebration and appreciation need to be built into workflow and company culture, so it doesn't just depend on the whim of the founder or someone else remembering to do it.

☐ Systems, money, and support all need to be handled thoughtfully so that "hustle" culture and unhealthy deadlines don't creep in, and so your team can work healthy amounts and still care for their families.

Consider alternative work schedules, twenty- to thirty-hour weeks considered as full time, and working to projects rather than to "work hours" unless necessary.

☐ Consider team trips, retreats, or other perks if your company revenue can support it.

☐ As founder/owner, make sure you are enjoying yourself, working reasonable hours, and appreciating all that is being accomplished.

Printed in the USA
CPSIA information can be obtained
at www.ICGtesting.com
LVHW090743140923
758113LV00006B/66